GHOST
STORIES
of
Saskatchewan

For Dennis.

Your love and support made this possible;

I am grateful for you every day

of my life.

GHOST STORIES
of
Saskatchewan

JO-ANNE CHRISTENSEN

HOUNSLOW

Ghost Stories of Saskatchewan

Hounslow Press
A member of the Dundurn Group

Publisher: Anthony Hawke
Design: Andy Tong
Editor: Nadine Stoikoff
Printer: Transcontinental Printing Inc.
Photographs: All photographs are by Jo-Anne Christensen with the exception of the photograph on page 91 which is by Leslie Charlton.

Canadian Cataloguing in Publication Data

Christensen, Jo-Anne
  Ghost stories of Saskatchewan

Includes bibliographical references.
ISBN 0-88882-177-8

1. Ghosts – Saskatchewan. I. Title.

BF1472.C3C57 1995   133.I'097124 C95-930613-7

Second printing: November, 1995
Third printing: November, 1996
Fourth printing: February, 1998
Fifth printing: December, 1998
Sixth printing: September, 1999

Publication was assisted by the **Canada Council**, the **Book Publishing Industry Development Program** of the **Department of Canadian Heritage**, the **Ontario Arts Council**, and the **Ontario Publishing Centre** of the **Ministry of Culture, Tourism and Recreation**.

Care has been taken to trace the ownership of copyright material used in this book. The author and the publisher welcome any information enabling them to rectify any references or credit in subsequent editions.

Printed and bound in Canada

Hounslow Press
8 Market Street
Suite 200
Toronto, Ontario, Canada
M5E 1M6

Hounslow Press
73 Lime Walk
Headington, Oxford
England
OX3 7AD

Hounslow Press
2250 Military Road
Tonawanda, NY
U.S.A. 14150

Contents

ACKNOWLEDGMENTS

The writing of this book was made possible by the expertise, kindness and generosity of many people. On numerous occasions, I have been overwhelmed by the assistance and encouragement offered me, and the time has come to express my gratitude.

To Tony Hawke, my publisher, thank you for this wonderful opportunity! Your support and benevolence has not gone unnoticed.

To Leslie Charlton, my industrious research assistant, thank you for your efforts, your enthusiasm and your fine taste in road-trip cookies.

Many thanks to my patient brother-in-law, Ed Shappka, who loaned me his photographic equipment and to date, hasn't even asked for its return!

To Lyla Charlton, I offer my gratitude for the warm hospitality and magnificent deep-dish plum pie; in light of Dave Charlton's subliminal contribution, I can only say "SON"!

My family and friends, as always, were first-class cheerleaders. Gerry, Marty, Tracy, Auntie Joan, Stella and all the Shappka family, I thank you. My husband, Dennis Shappka, frequently banished anxieties and provided valuable perspective and input; he deserves public acknowledgment. And special mentions go to my brothers Darwin (known in certain literary circles as "research boy") and Jeff (still the friendliest ghostie I know) – I love you and thank you for just being there.

Loved ones can always be counted on for support, but in the course of my research, I had the good fortune to also encounter dozens of kind and helpful strangers. Some requested anonymity, and I respect their wishes and offer my gratitude. The others, I wish to publicly thank. They include Cathie Adams, Broadview Library; Frank Anderson, Gopher Books, Saskatoon; Anne Antoshewski, Weirdale;

Gloria Bourassa, Bienfait Town Office; Maud Brown, Unity, Peggy Brunsdon, Manager, Government House Heritage Property; Shirley Corkish, Wawota and District Museum; Bernie Eresman, Moose Jaw Public Library; Vera Falk, Wilson Museum Inc., Dundurn; Katherine Falkner, CKOM Radio, Saskatoon; Dave Geary, Saskatoon; Gertrude B. Hillier, Southey and District Museum; Lois Holcomb, CKBI Radio, Prince Albert; Bruce Johnstone, *The Regina Leader-Post;* Gisele Lemire, Edmonton; Lila Martinson, Assiniboia and District Historical Society; Mary O. McLean, Saskatoon; Hazel J. McCloskey, Prairie West Historical Society; Lisa Monk, Edmonton, Carole Naylor, John M. Cuelenaere Library, Prince Albert; Norm Park, *The Estevan Mercury;* Tom Roberts, CBC-FM Radio, La Ronge; Greg Salmers, Estevan Public Library; Sue Sandrey, *The Regina Leader-Post;* Brent Shepherd, CJVR Radio, Melfort; Edmonton author and folklorist Michael Taft; Penny Werle, Saskatoon Public Library; and Dr. Buddy Wynn, University of Regina.

A special thanks is owed to author Barbara Smith, a remarkable talent and good friend who was endlessly generous with her counsel and encouragement. Without you, Barbara, this book never would have happened.

INTRODUCTION

Mention to someone that you're writing a book about Saskatchewan ghost stories, and you will invariably be asked this question:

"Why Saskatchewan?"

Saskatchewanians asked; people from other provinces asked; when I did radio or television interviews, it was always the first item on the agenda.

I suppose I know why. After all, we're talking about a farming and mining province, a *sensible* province, distinguishable only (according to one smirking comedian) as "the easiest province to draw."

But I know differently. I know that Saskatchewan is a *haunted* province.

The fact is that where there are people, there are ghosts. An earthbound spirit is as likely to haunt a grain elevator as a castle; *more* likely, if grain elevators are what make up the landscape. Dramatic events will leave impressions on the open prairies as assuredly as on the misty moors, and Saskatchewan has a vivid history that's bound to have left its psychic mark.

If you have an interest in ghost stories, perhaps it's time to taste the local variety.

These are the ghost stories of Saskatchewan. Enjoy.

An Unlucky House

IN THE YEAR THAT JOEL SCOTT LIVED IN THIS HOUSE, HE BECAME
OBSESSED WITH ITS DARK HISTORY.

Which came first, the chicken or the egg?

*Many haunted houses invite this style of speculation. Does a powerfully
negative energy exist in a house because a number of terrible things have
happened there, or does the negativity cause the tragedy? This story left me
wondering*

When Joel Scott moved into the charming two-storey house
on Regina's College Avenue, he was a hopeful young newly-
wed. It was the spring of 1976. In May of 1977, Joel moved
out, with his sixteen-month-old marriage in crumbling ruins.

A sad story, but not so unusual; unless you take into account that
Joel claimed the house he and his wife lived in contributed to the
destruction of the relationship – and that perhaps his marriage wasn't
the building's first victim. This was a house with a morbid history, and

in his one-year stay, Joel was to discover much about it.

The day the Scotts moved in, there was a small foreshadow of things to come. As they made trip after trip through the front door with their belongings, Joel noticed something lying by the side of the house. It turned out to be a rubber sink-stopper. He assumed it must have fallen from the second-storey bathroom window, and on his next trip into the house, replaced it on the counter by the sink.

A few minutes later, the stopper was again on the ground outside the house.

Joel believed his wife must have been playing a prank. Once more, he returned the stopper to the sink, this time closing the bathroom window for good measure.

The remainder of the afternoon was spent indoors, as the newly-weds busily arranged furniture and personal belongings in their new home. Late in the day, Joel stepped outside for some fresh air, and was a little annoyed to find the bathroom sink-stopper in the grass beside the house for the third time.

Joel made a comment to his wife, but she claimed to know nothing about the wandering rubber stopper. As a curious but unimportant event in the midst of a hectic day, the incident was, for a time, forgotten.

The Scotts settled comfortably into their new home, but before long, they were confronted with other mysteries.

Their sleep would often be interrupted by the sound of breaking glass, but when Joel investigated the main floor, expecting to confront vandals, he found nothing.

When the couple's backs were turned, a thirty-pound potted plant that was in the living room would reposition itself in the dining room, approximately eight feet away. Smaller items would move on their own, as well; sometimes disappearing for a period of time, then reappearing in a different location. The travelling sink-stopper was a frequent puzzler.

Doors at the Scott residence were another anomaly, opening and closing by themselves, and the electrical system seemed to function independently, as well. On one occasion, Joel and his wife were visiting their neighbours, when they happened to glance out the window. Across the street, lights were going on and off in various rooms of their own house. They rushed home immediately, only to find everything as they had left it. The house was empty, and the only burning lights were those that they had left on before going out.

It was also impossible to explain the drastic temperature drop in one particular part of the bathroom. The "cold column" was a two- to three-foot-square area that extended from floor to ceiling. Tested with a thermometer, it appeared to be colder than the rest of the bathroom by approximately ten degrees Celsius. The phenomenon only took place on certain days, however, making it difficult to account for in any rational manner.

Somehow, the unexplainable events of the Scott household became public knowledge. Joel and his wife began losing their privacy, as their home became a local curiosity.

Showing no respect for the occupants of the "haunted house," ghost-hunters frequently trampled flower beds and peered in the windows. Strangers showed up at all hours, wanting to take pictures and hoping to see a ghost. One couple even offered the Scotts two hundred dollars for the opportunity to stay overnight in their home.

Sensing this kind of financial opportunity, profiteers came out of the woodwork. Joel reported receiving letters from a number of mystics, parapsychologists and psychic phenomena experts. Some showed legitimate professional interest; others clearly wanted to make a quick, exploitive buck. The publicity even prompted a local radio personality to interview Joel in his home, in the hopes that some supernatural noises would be evident on the tape. None were.

Joel Scott may have been inconvenienced and annoyed by the public's fascination, but he understood it completely. After having lived in the house a few months, he was completely intrigued by the secrets it held. In the August 25, 1979 edition of *The Regina Leader-Post*, he told reporter Bruce Johnstone that he found himself becoming infatuated with the house and its strange events. In fact, he became so obsessed with telling friends and acquaintances each new discovery about the house's horrible history, he admitted later, "I realize now, people must have thought I was crazy."

Crazy or not, Joel Scott began to piece together a pattern of tragedy in connection with his home.

In 1973 or '74, a young girl who lived in the house had collapsed and died of a seizure in the upstairs bathroom. Her prone body was discovered in the spot where the cold column later existed.

The next unlucky tenants were Saskatchewan's deputy minister of social services, Hubert A. Prefontaine and his family. As well as being a popular politician, Prefontaine was a skilled pilot, and at 8:45 PM on January 22, 1975, he left St. Andrew's satellite field of the Winnipeg airport in a single-engine Piper Cherokee. One hour later, Prefontaine made his last radio contact when he routinely requested clearance through the Brandon control area. Another hour after that, when the plane did not arrive in Regina as expected, the Canadian Armed Forces search and rescue unit in Edmonton was contacted. The next morning, George Fuller, a CP Rail signal maintainer at Balgonie, discovered the wreckage.

Hubert Prefontaine and his wife, Carol, were both dead. Miraculously, their two youngest daughters, aged one and a half and four years, survived the crash and a night of sub-zero temperatures with minor injuries. Four older daughters had not been with their parents on that fateful night; according to newspaper reports, they heard the horrible news at the family home on College Avenue.

In his *Leader-Post* interview, Joel Scott intimated that there were another two deaths connected to the house, and that the circumstances were "unusual" and "mysterious." It is not known if he discovered any more details on past tenants, but one thing is certain: the newest casualty in the College Avenue house was to be the Scott's marriage.

The first year of marriage is often difficult, and Joel Scott and his wife surely dealt with some additional stresses. They unwillingly sacrificed a great deal of privacy, when the publicity was at its peak. Joel's wife didn't share his new and intense interest in the house and the unusual phenomenon. And finally, there is the possibility that the couple's relationship may have been sabotaged directly by supernatural forces in the house.

Joel Scott contradicted himself interestingly when describing the disintegration of his marriage. "The stress and tension of the marriage breaking down may have caused some of the kinetic energy in the house," he said at one time, paradoxically adding later that the mysterious happenings in the house, "definitely contributed to the downfall of the marriage."

Whether they created the negative energy in the house or fell victim to it, the Scotts were heading for divorce court when they left the College Avenue house in May of 1977.

Once he had distanced himself from the house, Joel began to wonder if there weren't rational explanations for much of what he experienced. The forty-year-old wiring might have accounted for some flickering lights, and perhaps the settling foundation of such an old structure could explain the odd closing door. For many, however, it is easier to believe in ghosts than in Joel Scott's eventual theory that mysteriously disappearing or moving objects were the work of a mischievous neighbourhood child who either had availed himself of a key, or snuck in secretly through the coal chute.

Even years later, when Joel Scott was attempting to pin natural explanations to each seemingly supernatural occurrence, he admitted that in many cases, it seemed impossible. He also spoke to the *Leader-*

Post of the intangible dread the house gave him; claiming that it had "bad vibes," and cursed its occupants with "bad luck."

Despite these negative associations, when Joel left the College Avenue house, he took with him a small souvenir.

It was the bathroom sink-stopper. And in Joel Scott's new home, it stayed put.

A Warning from Doc's Wife

Broadview is one of Saskatchewan's "CPR towns"; a place that wouldn't exist, had it not been for the railroad. The Canadian Pacific Railway virtually created the town, and was its biggest employer until the late '60s, when cutbacks began.

Ironically, in this story shared by Saskatoon author Frank Anderson, one of the trains that gave Broadview its very life's blood nearly ended the life of one of its important citizens.

"Back in the 1920s, our family lived in a two-storey white house, right beside a CPR underpass. Doc lived on a hill, about 100 yards from us."

Perhaps because of this proximity, and the fact that both men were university graduates – rarer, in those days – "Doc" was a close friend to Frank Anderson's foster father. Frank was only about eight years old at the time, but enjoyed being in the periphery of the relationship.

"Doc was a very important person to me," said Frank, "even though I no longer remember his name." He does remember the doctor's neat appearance; that of a conservative dresser who wore glasses and favoured a short white goatee. He remembers that the man owned a radio, and let young Frank listen to it, on occasion. And he remembers that Doc was a widower.

In 1918, Spanish influenza devastated the entire world, killing 21 million people; nearly the number of casualties suffered in the first world war. The little town of Broadview was not spared. Many soldiers who arrived home from Europe were unwitting carriers of the virus, and eventually, a second mortuary had to be set up to deal with the overwhelming number of deaths.

Many of the disease's victims were young, vigorous adults. Doc's wife, who was likely exposed to the flu more than the average person due to her husband's profession, was among them. Never remarrying, Doc continued his medical practice in Broadview.

One night, some years later, there was a call for emergency medical attention at a house a few miles west of town. It was a dismally rainy and foggy night, but Doc tossed his black bag in the Model T Ford,

In the late 1920s, one of the trains that rumbled along these tracks in Broadview would have taken the life of a young doctor had it not been for a timely and quite ghostly warning.

cranked the engine to life and ventured out on slippery roads.

"Now, visibility wasn't good at the best of times," Frank explained. "The railway curves used to be shorter; the railway cuts, not as wide, and about four miles west of town, the rails took a sharp curve through a deep cut in a hill. At this same spot, the gravel road turned south very sharply, across the tracks." It would have been difficult to cross the tracks safely in fair weather. Doc was driving in the night rain.

It happened that Doc was destined to round that corner at the precise moment that a train approached the crossing. Fortunately, a guardian spirit had another destiny in mind. Frank Anderson still remembers how the amazed doctor told the story.

"He said his wife appeared suddenly, sitting on the hood of his Ford, urgently warning him to stop. He skidded to a halt a few feet from the crossing, just as the train thundered by."

Was it truly a ghost, or a strong sense of intuition, manifesting itself in a recognizable form? No one will ever know, but Frank knows what Doc escaped, that night.

"A short while later, a local man's car was struck by a CPR train. My foster mother reluctantly allowed me to go downtown and see the damaged vehicle, sitting on top of a dray." Solemnly, he adds, "It was my first knowledge of violent death."

It might have been his second, were it not for a timely warning from the doctor's dead wife.

An Unseen Playmate

"It was a dark and stormy night ...."

I've spent many enjoyable evenings that way. Telling ghost stories is one of the most entertaining ways to survive a power outage or pass the time around a campfire.

One August night, my husband and I were sharing a holiday trailer with my brother and his girlfriend, Leslie. We were tucked into our beds, in complete darkness, trying to scare each other to sleep.

Everyone shared a spooky story, and the point seemed to be to make each tale more fearsome and dramatic than the previous one. It was Leslie's quiet account, however – told with such sincerity, it was impossible to disbelieve – that stayed on my mind.

"Something happened to me once," she said, "that convinced me there are things out there we just don't understand."

Leslie Charlton remembers the summer of 1978 very well. Not because she was getting ready to return to school as a "cool" grade six student – although she was. Not because she had begun to notice boys as more than just annoyances – although she had. Leslie remembers that summer for another reason. An unexplainable one.

Summer vacation for Leslie and her friends meant falling into a comfortable routine. The days were spent hanging around the house, seeking refuge from the Regina heat, "waiting for the Dickie Dee man," as Leslie puts it. Evenings were unfailingly devoted to "swing tag," a favourite game in the neighbourhood.

Leslie explains swing tag as being a creative variation of the "tag-you're-it" game that everyone grew up with. Four people are on the swings, and are not allowed to touch their feet to the ground. A fifth person is "it," and is forced to stay outside an imaginary boundary drawn around the poles of the swing set. Whoever is "it" has to tag one of the players, without crossing the boundary, to gain a turn on the swing.

"From grade one to grade seven, we did that all summer," Leslie said, adding that they always played at the school playground, across the street from her mother's house.

ONE HOT, STILL SUMMER EVENING IN THIS REGINA PLAYGROUND,
THE THIRD SWING FROM THE RIGHT (SET IN MOTION BEFORE THIS
PICTURE WAS TAKEN) MOVED DELIBERATELY FOR SEVERAL MINUTES,
AS THOUGH IT CARRIED AN INVISIBLE RIDER.

The evening that Leslie remembers so well had offered no relief from the oppressive heat of the day. The swing tag game lasted until after sunset, and even then, the air remained heavy and still. Leslie was on one of the middle swings, tucking her feet in carefully, so as not to be "tagged," when she noticed something unusual.

In the next section of the swing structure, one of the deserted swings was beginning to move. Not waving or swaying a bit, but moving deliberately back and forth, and gaining more height with every pass. The chains hung taut and stayed parallel. The canvas seat appeared to be weighted down. The swing moved higher and higher, impossibly, on its own. Most interestingly, the vacant swings on either side of it remained perfectly still, apparently unaffected by the invisible force.

"I was the first one to say anything," said Leslie. "I stopped and put my feet down on the ground and said ... well, I probably swore," she admitted, "because we swore all the time at that age, but I said 'Did anyone else see that?' The guy right beside me said he saw it too. Then we all turned and watched this thing swinging back and forth by itself."

Just as it began gradually, the swing slowed itself down before coming to a complete stop. The group continued to watch it intently, but no one dared go near it. What they did do was talk about what happened.

"We had to talk about something, so we were trying to believe it was some kind of contraption. We thought someone was behind a car with a piece of fishing line, making it go back and forth. Someone said 'wind,' but there was no way it was wind, because all the rest of the swings were perfectly still."

Finally, before leaving the playground, one of the boys mustered enough bravery to walk around the affected swing, checking for wires or strings. There was nothing.

The hour was late, and the group scattered, everyone eager for the bright, reassuring lights of home. They spoke of the incident later, but only to each other. "I didn't even tell my mother until years and years later," said Leslie, "because it was just too weird, you know?"

She still remembers her friends' final consensus, after ruling out ordinary causes. "We thought some little kid had fallen off the swing and hit his head and died. Perished right there in the playground."

And what does she think now?

"I don't know what it was. But I *do* know it wasn't wind, and I know that it wasn't someone playing a trick."

For all anyone does know, there's just a lonely little spirit in a deserted Regina playground, waiting for someone to start another lively game of swing tag.

[T]here were some wonderful ghost stories surrounding an old abandoned farm home near my home town that kept us in complete bewilderment for years ...

A person or two supposedly died mysteriously in that house. It then had to be abandoned by its next owners because of the ghosts, and was never lived in again ... or so the story went ...

I returned to that old home town a few years ago and drove by that hill not too far from the highway ... and got goose bumps.

Real good ghost stories can do that to you, even when you are an adult.

Norm Park
The Estevan Mercury
July 1994

Mystery at the Moose Head

A PARTIAL VIEW OF THE SECOND-FLOOR NIGHTCLUB IN THE
MOOSE HEAD INN; THE ROOM WHERE DOORS CRASHED OPEN,
LIGHTS FLASHED ON AND OFF, AND INCREDIBLE "BOOMING"
NOISES ORIGINATED.

On several occasions, while interviewing for this book, I was strongly impressed by the conviction and credibility of the people who shared their stories.

Never more, however, than with Dale Orsted, the owner of a nightclub and restaurant in Kenosee Lake. Here was a sensible, unflappable business-man who, after examining every natural alternative, had to conclude that he was sharing his home and workplace with something quite unnatural.

His matter-of-fact account of events made me think that even a person who didn't believe in ghosts would find it impossible to disbelieve Dale.

One of the first strange things to happen, happened to Jeff Stephen. He was, at that time, manager of the Moose Head Inn in Kenosee Lake. Jeff needed to replace one of the bottles at the bar, and had gone downstairs, through the darkened restaurant, to the small room where the liquor was stored.

Dale Orsted, the owner, was giving me a tour of the restaurant as he shared the story. "The Porthole," with its obviously nautical theme, is nestled in the lower floor of the three-storey building. The heavy wood decor is enhanced dramatically by the fact that there is no natural light in the room. Jeff's experience was very likely heightened by this same fact; for when the restaurant is closed, and the switches turned off, not a ray of light penetrates the dark.

"We don't always bother to turn on the lights," Dale explained, "because we know where everything is, in here. We could find our way around blindfolded." This is what Jeff was doing, weaving deftly between the tables in a completely darkened room. When he reached the liquor storage area on the opposite side, however, he needed to see the labels on the bottles. He reached around the doorway, feeling the wall for the light switch.

That's when something felt *him*.

Later, Jeff described it as a cold hand that touched his wrist and ran lightly up his arm. The sensation rattled him so thoroughly, he forgot the task at hand and hastened back across the pitch-black restaurant and upstairs to the nightclub.

He arrived back at the bar, refusing to explain why he hadn't brought the necessary bottle, and unwilling to make another trip. Dale now recalls that it was a couple of weeks before Jeff even spoke of his experience. At that, he found the incident so unsettling, he didn't want to talk about it much.

Ironically, unsettling incidents were soon to become the number one topic of discussion at this popular nightclub.

Originally, it was Grandison Hall, a teen dance club built in 1968 by Archibald Grandison and his wife. It was a late-in-life project for this couple; they were in their sixties when they began. By the time Dale Orsted was old enough to attend teen dances at Kenosee Lake's most happening establishment, "Grandy" and his wife were well into their seventies. According to Dale, it didn't stop them from enjoying what they did.

"The place was big-time popular, and they'd ... almost with canes, you know ... walk up to the stage and thank everybody for coming out.

SCENIC KENOSEE LAKE, IN MOOSE MOUNTAIN PROVINCIAL PARK.
IT'S A PEACEFUL SETTING, FOR THOSE WHO DON'T DEAL WITH THE
RESIDENT GHOST.

And all the best bands were here; Streetheart, and Harlequin, and Loverboy. Anyone that was big, they had them here for their dances."

Unfortunately, Mr. Grandison's health began failing by 1978, and the hall was sold in March of the following year. Eventually renamed the "Moose Head Inn," the establishment changed hands throughout the eighties.

In 1989, the Moose Head was once again for sale, and this time, Dale Orsted was the prospective buyer. Having always lived in the area, Dale knew that this was a successful business. He was also fairly sure that a few changes could make it even more successful. The sale went ahead, and Dale took possession in March of 1990.

The three floors of the Moose Head Inn seemed to meet all of Dale's business and personal needs. The first floor was a cozy dining room; the second floor, a cabaret; and the third floor provided office space and a conveniently functional, if somewhat cramped, apartment. Dale moved in, made himself comfortable, and commenced work.

Renovations started on the second floor, in the nightclub. Hoping to update the look of the place, Dale had new bars built and changed the location of the deejay booth. Almost immediately thereafter, the confusing incidents began.

"Things would go missing," said Dale, "and come back two or three weeks later, to the same spot. I'd have people looking for the stuff, and *know* it wasn't there. And noises. I'd sit up here [in the apartment] and hear almost a banging ... like someone was trying to break in. Only, we'd listen for an hour, an hour and a half ... so he was a pretty slow burglar, if he was coming in."

Dale was often certain that there was a burglar in the club, however. On several occasions, he was convinced enough to phone the police.

"They'd come and check every inch out, and find nothing," he said. "Then it might happen again, after they'd leave."

Dale was worried enough to call the police "at least four or five times," he said, adding, "every time they come they've got their guns out, looking for the bad guys ... and then you feel stupid."

Embarrassment didn't stop Dale from taking extra security measures. The missing items in the club had him speculating that one of the previous owner's employees had a set of keys; so every lock in the building was replaced. The continuing late-night noises prompted him to install security cameras and motion detectors. Every precaution had been taken, yet nothing changed.

Items still went missing. Dale and his girlfriend were still awakened by loud banging sounds, coming from the cabaret. Eventually, they began to suspect that they weren't dealing with entirely earthly matters.

"One time," he said, "we had the phone book out, calling the police, and a gust of wind blew the pages of the phone book shut." The call was eventually made, and as usual, the police found nothing out of the ordinary. Dale's girlfriend might have reported differently, though; she was in the apartment when loud footsteps on the stairs had her thinking that Dale was bringing the officers up to talk to her. In fact, Dale and the police were outside, searching in vain for some footprints in the fresh snow, while the door at the bottom of the stairway remained securely locked.

On another evening, Dale captured the disturbing sounds on one of his surveillance video tapes.

"It was definitely inside the building," he said of the noise, adding, "It was more like an energy bang ... like when a bubble bursts, or a balloon pops." Dale saved the tape, but was unable to find it later.

The noises eventually went away; and if small items were found missing, it happened so infrequently that it was easily dismissed as human forgetfulness. Business was good, and life at the Moose Head Inn became calm.

It was a brief respite.

In February of 1992, Dale decided to remove the old carpeting from the cabaret floor. It was frayed and worn, probably as old as the building, and it needed to go. Dale and Jeff put in a late night ripping the old rug from the floorboards, then retired to the apartment. At 4:00 AM, they were shocked into consciousness.

Dale, Jeff and Dale's girlfriend all awoke to violent crashing noises coming from the floor below. With no idea of what they might face, Dale and Jeff bravely ventured downstairs to investigate. Jeff insured himself by carrying a length of steel pipe, but didn't need it, for once the two men were in the nightclub, the sounds stopped. The minute they settled back into the apartment, however, it began again, "loud as a car crash," in Jeff's words. It was a frustrating cycle that was to continue every night for the next two weeks, and sporadically, for months.

When the deafening noises resumed, other unexplainable things began to happen, as well. The Moose Head's newly installed motion detector was tripped when no one was in the building. The dishwasher by the bar once turned itself on for approximately ten seconds, when no one had touched it. And several times, in the early morning hours, when the club was closed and staff members were relaxing with a drink, steel doors outfitted with emergency panic hardware would fly open with a huge bang, then just as alarmingly, slam shut. According to Dale, it was an effective way to empty a room.

"Usually," he notes drily, "people are gone, two minutes later."

The electric lights also acted autonomously. Dale and Jeff would routinely turn off all the cabaret lights at the end of the evening, and return later to find that some had been switched back on. One time, Dale had just taken care of this task, and barely turned his back, when he heard the light switch click into position behind him. He turned around to see the bar lights that he had just shut off glowing defiantly.

What Dale Orsted refers to as his most frightening experience at the Moose Head Inn happened in February of '92, on the evening the carpet renovations were complete.

"We were sitting here in the apartment, watching TV. From the adjoining room, suddenly there was this very eerie moaning sound. It sounded as if someone was in extreme pain, and lasted for about ten seconds. We just sat there, pretending we didn't hear it. I was scared, and my girlfriend, you could see her eyes just popping out. But we didn't mention a word until later that night."

Around four o'clock the next morning, after Dale and his girlfriend managed to get to sleep, the activity resumed. Again, it was a crashing noise, "as loud and violent as a head-on collision," but this incident differed. All the previous noises had come from the nightclub, downstairs;

THE MOOSE HEAD INN IS KENOSEE LAKE'S POPULAR CHOICE FOR DINING, DANCING AND HAUNTING.

this one seemed to be right outside the apartment door.

The sound created enough physical impact to break dishes that were sitting in the kitchen sink. The faucet turned on by itself, and water began gushing down the drain. Dale and his girlfriend spent several hours shaking in fright and waiting for the sun to rise. When it did, she moved out.

On February 1, 1992, the *Winnipeg Free Press* carried an advertisement that read "Haunted houses investigated, ten years experience." The ad sparked the curiosity of a reporter, who followed up with a story in the *Winnipeg Sun*. That same story was picked up by a Saskatchewan paper, and read with great interest by Dale Orsted's girlfriend.

The original ad had been placed by Roy Bauer and Chris Rutkowski of Spectre Paranormal Investigations. The young woman knew that Dale was near the end of his rope; he had even talked of simply walking away from the business. Thinking that this might be the kind of help he needed, she called the number, and ended up talking to Roy Bauer about her experiences at the Moose Head.

Bauer seemed interested in the case, and he was not alone. When he visited the Moose Head Inn in May, he had a reporter and film crew from CBC's *Newsmagazine* in tow. *The Regina Leader-Post* had recently run a story on the Moose Head, and now it seemed that everyone wanted to know what was haunting this popular club.

From a little investigation of his own, Dale thought he might know. He believed that the second floor of the building had originally been part of an old country church, near Kipling. There were rumours that decades earlier, a priest had hanged himself in its bell tower.

Roy Bauer dismissed the idea, after discovering that the building material in question came not from the church itself, but from a nearby community hall that belonged to the church. That left him looking for another ghostly "suspect," and he settled on Archibald Grandison. Bauer interviewed Mrs. Grandison in front of CBC's camera, and began to formulate a theory.

His feeling was that Grandison Hall had been a major accomplishment for Archibald, particularly since he had taken the project on so late in life. His sudden decline in health hadn't allowed him to give the hall up gradually, and so, after his death in 1983, his spirit was drawn back there.

For years, he caused no problems; then came Dale Orsted's renovations. Roy Bauer speculated that Mr. Grandison didn't appreciate seeing his hard work torn apart by strangers, and began making his presence known. In a follow-up report to Dale and Jeff, Bauer suggested that they "reconsider making any major renovations in the future, unless the phenomenon has stopped completely."

Bauer also suggested the playing of a customized audio tape, in which he would attempt to communicate with Mr. Grandison. Three weeks later, in another correspondence, he offered a more drastic piece of advice. "I strongly feel that if the audio tape does not work," he wrote, "the only way you will be able to get rid of the problem is by tearing down the Inn and rebuilding it from scratch."

Dale Orsted had yet to be completely convinced, however, that the ghost was Mr. Grandison. A bit more of his own research had revealed some other interesting possibilities.

It turned out that there had been a terrible car accident, some years earlier, where two or three young people were killed, on the way home from the hall. Dale noted that with interest, reminded of how so many of the unexplained noises sounded like a violent, head-on collision.

Supernatural stories connected to the church continued to find their way to Dale, as well. There were rumours of people dying unexpectedly, just a short time after visiting the church. According to legend, vehicles would stall on the road that ran in front of it, refusing to restart until they were pushed past the church yard. People claimed that the building glowed eerily at night, and that some visitors returned to their vehicle to discover a freshly cut rose lying on the seat.

The most likely suspect, however, was far less dramatic. When Dale learned of a quiet man who had been associated with the Moose Head Inn in the '80s, and allegedly died believing that his contribution to the business had not been appreciated, he sensed that he may have found his ghost.

Strengthening Dale's theory was a list of "clues" provided by a Winnipeg psychic. The woman had never been to the Moose Head, but provided pages of information about the spirit that roamed the cabaret, and about the building itself. Her impressions of the Inn and its contents were so accurate that it lent credibility to her description of the ghost. And her description of the ghost was more of a custom fit for Dale's suspect than it was for Archibald Grandison.

For most people, however, the identity of the ghost was of considerably less interest than the validity of it. Although Dale had never actively sought any of the media attention, some people, including reporters he had been kind enough to cooperate with, were cynically suggesting that his stories were nothing more than a publicity stunt. Dale scoffed at the idea, saying that the Moose Head Inn was thriving before the rumour got out.

"I don't think it brought us business, because we were always busy. It just changed the types of questions that the staff got," he explained, adding that after a point, it was a hindrance. "It got so that every two minutes, there was somebody else wanting to talk about it." In an effort to answer their questions, he began printing his daily restaurant specials on the reverse side of the photocopied ghost story. And in the spirit of fun, the nightclub was staffed by "ghost-bouncers." But Dale insisted that if he had created a gimmick, he would have created one that was easier to live with.

"A lot of people thought it was a good promotion scam," he said, shaking his head, "but at four o'clock in the morning, I didn't think so." His detractors should have noted that for some time, Dale chose to commute from distant Estevan, rather than live with what they referred to as his "publicity stunt."

There were also sceptics who, while never doubting Dale Orsted's integrity, had a hard time believing his supernatural explanations. Non-believing staff members, however, almost always changed their minds after having a strange experience or two.

One of the converts, a kitchen worker, was interviewed for CBC's

Newsmagazine. He claimed to have been sceptical about the ghost, until he witnessed the heavy kitchen cooler door, usually kept in place by a latch and air pressure, open and close on its own.

"It's hard NOT to say you believe in ghosts!" he exclaimed. "I mean, the cooler opened and shut! There's *no way* that cooler can open and shut! I was *there*!"

According to Dale Orsted, most staff members have encountered the entity at one time or another. "And you can tell if they're telling the truth," he said. "Ones that just want to jump on the bandwagon, they don't have the same look in their eyes. When someone's just had an experience, you look in their eyes, and there's fear."

One young woman who worked for Dale claimed no fear of ghosts. She, her mother, and her grandmother all had some degree of psychic ability, and the entire family was very accepting of paranormal activity. Still, she was notably distressed after one experience in the nightclub.

"This was late at night, and we were closed," said Dale. "Now, it seems to hang out in the girls' bathroom, and this girl was in there all by herself. Suddenly, all the doors on the stalls are banging open and closed, and all the toilets start flushing. When we got back, she was just shaking in the corner, waiting for us." Dale added that "if it happened once, you'd maybe doubt it, but we've had three or four girls say the same story."

Recently, the activity tends to be much less dramatic. For a special long weekend event, Dale and Jeff temporarily moved the bars into the centre of the nightclub, creating a stand-up area. A week later, the downstairs restaurant was still plagued by the phantom sounds of furniture being dragged across the floor above.

Deadbolts that have been slid into position are occasionally found unlocked, these days, and every once in a while, Dale will hear the doorknob to his apartment turn slightly, as if someone's testing it from the other side.

These events would be more than enough to frighten most people, but after what Dale Orsted has experienced, this is a state of calm. While there's no doubt that he prefers it, he does have a strange reason for missing the phenomenon.

"You tend to want it to come back, because after you're away from it for awhile, you start to doubt yourself again. When it's happening, you're sure that nothing's ever gonna let you forget that it happened ... but after awhile you just want to get reinforced."

If there is some part of Dale that wishes for a repeat performance, there is a more sensible part of him that certainly does not. His current schedule confirms that. He takes his time with the closing duties these days, after everyone's left the club. He has a nightcap and putters around. By the time he goes to bed, it's dawn, and the window of opportunity for any supernatural activity has passed. But avoidance wasn't always so easy.

"When I first moved here, there was no TV after midnight, but now there is one twenty-four-hour channel, Yorkton. Before, I'd go to bed, turn the snow on, turn it up loud and try to cover whatever was happening."

If anything does happen, Dale is now dealing with it on his own. His girlfriend never did move back in. Jeff Stephen, Dale's long-time manager and friend, recently married and left the business entirely. So, after a period of several months when absolutely no one would risk living in the Moose Head's third-floor apartment, Dale moved back in, by himself.

Imagine him alone, late at night ...

With the television on ...

Listening and waiting.

It's really just another classic tale ... of things that go 'bump' in the nightclub.

House with a History

If you take a walking tour of Saskatoon, the sights may include a distinctive three-storey apartment house at 844 Saskatchewan Crescent. The building has historical significance, but at least a few people find it fascinating for more recent, albeit lesser known, events.

It was 1911 when George E. McCraney and his wife, Elizabeth, built their grand new house on Saskatchewan Crescent. It was three storeys of handsome red brick; solid evidence of the success this couple was enjoying. George had been practising law since 1902 and at the young age of forty-three, had just been elected to his third term in the House of Commons. In the next decade, he would become beloved by the citizens of Saskatoon for his unselfish service in charities, church work and a variety of patriotic and educational causes. Then, at age fifty-two, just as many began thinking he would be Saskatchewan's next lieutenant-governor, George fell victim to apoplexy (the then-common term for a stroke) and died. His body was shipped back to the family burial plot in Ontario, but some people believe that his spirit remained on.

Elizabeth McCraney continued to live in the huge house until 1928. In '29, just before the depression, the building was converted into six separate suites, and renamed "The McDougal Apartments." Since then, a series of strange events have people wondering if the old McCraney house is, in fact, haunted.

In recent years, two young men were undoubtedly charmed by the character of the building when they decided to share one of its apartments. They were both lawyers, analytical to the core, so when odd things began to happen, they were determined to find rational explanations. Eventually, however, they were forced to wonder if such explanations existed. One of the fellows was quoted in a 1991 issue of *The Star Phoenix* as saying, "I'm not superstitious. But I can't explain some of the bizarre events."

Those "bizarre events" included icy cold breezes that would blow through the apartment, making the hair on the backs of their necks

THIS AGING BRICK BUILDING, NOW A SASKATOON APARTMENT
HOUSE, WAS ORIGINALLY HOME TO ONE OF THE PROVINCE'S ELITE
COUPLES; GEORGE AND ELIZABETH MCCRANEY.

stand on end. The one man, who claimed to be the soundest of sleepers, would awaken every morning at five o'clock. And a door that had been securely locked and chain-latched by one of the roommates was mysteriously ajar when the other returned home.

This particular ghost demonstrated a flair for dramatics, too. The one lawyer was sitting alone in the living room one evening, when he heard the strange sound of rushing air coming from down the hall. He bravely followed the noise into his roommate's bedroom, and was greeted with the sight of clothing flying out of the closet. A closer examination of the scene showed that the valve of a scuba tank being stored in the closet had opened, and was blowing the clothing around. No one, however, could explain how the valve opened.

There was a neighbour, as well, who reported awakening one night to the sound of dishes clattering in the kitchen. He investigated, and saw the apparition of a woman standing at the sink.

That particular incident may have fuelled the rumour that a woman was once killed in one of the upstairs suites. According to Saskatoon historians, however, the murder in question happened at another neighbourhood home. The one life we can be sure was cut short at 844 Saskatchewan Crescent was George McCraney's, and it's possible that to this day, he's reluctant to leave his precious home.

A Ghost in Rockglen

No more than one-half hour's drive from the U.S. border sits the small, quiet community of Rockglen, Saskatchewan. The perfect place to enjoy an idyllic and wholesome family life? ... Garth and Amy Harrison (pseudonyms) probably thought so. Whatever their reasons, in August of 1977, the Harrisons moved into a turn-of-the-century, three-bedroom ranch house outside of Rockglen. It appeared to be a comfortable home in which to start their family. They were soon to discover how deceiving appearances can be.

Amy recalls that her first "uncomfortable" incident in the house happened the first winter, after she and Garth moved in.

"There was a verandah on the front of the house that had been closed in, to make an extra room. That was where we kept the washer and dryer, right beside the doorway that led to the basement," Amy told me.

The doorway to the basement was, in fact, little more than a hole in the floor that had been covered by a board. On this particular day, as Amy transferred the wet laundry from the washer to the dryer, the board was slightly out of place, leaving an opening.

"I had this feeling," she told me, "that something was tugging on my pant-leg. I thought maybe it was caught on a nail, so I just gave my leg a shake." The moment she stopped moving, however, the sensation returned. Somewhat nonplussed, she hurriedly finished her chore and left the verandah-room. Once in another part of the house, the eerie feeling disappeared and so, soon after, did Amy's concern. She even forgot to mention the strange incident to Garth, and might have forgotten it entirely, had she not been reminded, days later.

She was reminded when Garth described having had the identical experience.

It was spooky, but the Harrisons did their best to explain such things away. Even when they couldn't, the most unsettling experiences would eventually fade into memory and lose their frightening power. And certainly, Amy and Garth had other things on their minds.

Two years after moving into the house, the Harrisons welcomed their first child, Dusty. A year later, twins Tessa and Tanya followed. Many experts in the field of parapsychology agree that children, who do not yet hold socialized beliefs of what is and isn't possible, tend to be more sensitive to unusual phenomenon. Because of their perceptiveness, youngsters may even have a catalytic influence on supernatural activity. Indeed, Amy estimates that "things really started to happen," when the twins were about eighteen months old.

Tessa and Tanya would frequently awaken, sobbing, in the middle of the night. Dusty began to suffer from graphic nightmares. The children began telling Amy and Garth that they saw "red eyes" staring at them from their bedroom window, and that sometimes there was someone in the bedroom with them. Dusty would frantically point at the "person," in an effort to convince his parents, but Amy and Garth could see no one.

The events may have been chalked up to childish imagination, but the elder Harrisons were having strange and frightening experiences of their own. The television began switching on and off, sans human intervention. Amy had the distinct feeling she was being watched, every day at 5:00 PM, as she fixed the family's dinner. Garth, who liked to listen to the stereo while he showered, could not explain how the volume would adjust itself wildly, when he was the only person in the house.

On one occasion, Garth was shaving in the bathroom when he glanced into the mirror and saw a bath towel flying toward the back of his head. Terrified, he spun around in time to see two more coming at him. Understandably, he left the house in a hurry. Admirably, he found the courage to eventually return.

Garth was also plagued by phantom sounds; footsteps, and the voice of an elderly man calling out to him. Each room he would follow the voice into would be predictably empty, however.

It was Amy who finally managed to see the presence, late one night as she went to check on her children.

"It was the grey shape of a man," she said. He appeared to her to be tall and thin, with his feet spread and his hands on his hips. The apparition disappeared in front of Amy's astonished eyes, but not all at once. He faded away gradually, top to bottom, starting with his head, and ending with his feet.

Frightened and at their wits' end, the Harrisons consulted a psychic. Without having seen their house, the woman was able to describe it perfectly. She also sensed a bit of unsavory history in connection with the building; apparently, a murder had taken place in the basement. Amy and Garth never researched the psychic's claim, but were very willing to take her advice regarding leaving the house. They started to make plans to move into a trailer on the same lot.

In November of 1986, they were ready to make the change, but not without taking some solemn precautions. The Harrisons had a Catholic priest come out; first, to bless the trailer, using salt and holy water, then, to bless each room in the newly vacant house, including the basement. Garth's one final preventative measure was to tear the house down and burn the remains.

And so, they thought, it had ended.

The Harrisons breathed a sigh of relief and began enjoying a peaceful life in their new home. Feeling quite confident that the events had become history, they even shared their story with a reporter from the *Saskatoon Star Phoenix,* for a Hallowe'en edition. That story resulted in a phone call from a Saskatoon woman, who recommended saying special prayers to keep the entity out of their new home. Amy politely thanked her for the advice, sure she would never need to use it. She was wrong.

Soon after the article appeared, Amy began hearing footsteps again; this time, in the loft of the barn. The noises were accompanied by the familiar feeling that something was there, something not good. She believed it to be the same unfriendly spirit that haunted the house.

"It's still around," she said, "it just moved to a different building."

And fortunately, that's where it remains. Amy has heeded the Saskatoon woman's advice, saying specific prayers to keep the Harrison home safe. It seems to be working, and most importantly, has given Amy a sense of being able to protect her family from other-worldly threats.

Hopefully, in the future, the Harrison home in Rockglen will remain as peaceful as it looks.

A Cold Reception at
Belle Plaine

THE FARM LAND SURROUNDING BELLE PLAINE IS ABOUT AS FLAT AND BALD AS PRAIRIE GETS. THERE IS NO NATURAL PROTECTION AGAINST THE COLD WINTER WINDS; A FACT THAT ONE SPECTRAL TROUBLE-MAKER WAS COUNTING ON.

One of the more popular theories explaining the presence of ghosts claims that they are spirits who simply don't understand they're dead. One Toronto parapsychologist believes that sixty percent of all hauntings fall into this category, and that it explains the majority of ghostly activity. The spirit sees itself as being real, and tries to function in a solid world without the appropriate tools. Adding to its frustration is the fact that no one seems to notice it. Therefore, many of the classic signs of a haunting – doors slamming, lights flickering, appliances turning on and off – may simply be a ghostly bid for attention.

In 1919, at a farm near Belle Plaine, a young family spent one cold winter with a spectre who knew exactly how to make them take notice.

The story goes that it was snowing and cold the November night that the family of four moved into the old farmhouse. Times were hard, and the young husband and father was happy to have found a job taking care of the place. The winter winds may have been blowing around them, but he knew his family would stay warm and comfortable in their cozy new two-storey home.

They were there four days, and had just settled in, when the husband and wife awoke one night to a terrible stomping sound in the kitchen. When the man went downstairs to investigate, he walked into a wall of icy air. At once, he realized why – the back door was standing wide open, admitting the bitterly cold night wind. The man shut and bolted the door, with a feeling of deja vu; he knew he had taken care of this chore earlier in the evening. When he turned back to the kitchen table to fetch the coal-oil lamp, the flame suddenly extinguished itself. The rest of the night was uneventful, but the man had already seen enough to believe his family was not alone in the old farmhouse.

It didn't take long before the ghost's activity was considered predictable. It seemed to confine its footsteps to the main floor of the house, and focused its attention almost exclusively on doors. There were some evenings when it seemed impossible to keep a single one shut. Inside, it was merely annoying, but the spirit's favourite activity was opening the outside door which, in the dead of one of Saskatchewan's harshest winters, was a serious problem. There were several nights when the family would awaken to a howling blizzard, go downstairs, and find snow drifting high into the kitchen.

An overnight guest once suggested that the house must have been built on a bit of a tilt, and that gravity was doing the rest. That couldn't explain the sturdy bolt on the outside door coming open however, or the mystery of the sliding door. There was an unusual sliding panel separating the living room from an unused addition to the house. It was always kept shut, and was such a sticky, stubborn contraption that a strong man would struggle to push it open. When the ghostly presence in the house felt like it, however, the panel would simply slide back into the wall, letting all the heat from the pot-belly stove escape into the empty addition.

In January and February of 1920, the temperatures dipped even lower and snow piled higher around the farmhouse. In an effort to insulate the front door that was never used, a day was spent plastering warm manure into every crack around the outside frame. That evening, the heavy clomping footsteps that were becoming familiar to the family were heard again, only this time, *outside* the house. The man rushed outside with a lantern and discovered that every single handful of manure that had been carefully packed against the door had vanished. He searched for some evidence of the spirit's stomping feet, and saw only a pristine blanket of fresh snow, stretching for miles.

That March, Belle Plaine saw the arrival of warmer temperatures, and the constant door opening became less of a problem. As it happened, the farm was sold that spring, and after just three and a half months, the family left to build a life in Moose Jaw. They later recalled that the timing may have been fortuitous. Only two weeks before the family left, the ghost began displaying more destructive behavior; specifically, one of the downstairs doors had been chopped at repeatedly with a hatchet.

Perhaps, without winter's cold as an ally, the ghost at Belle Plaine simply had to take greater measures to be paid the attention it craved.

Years after leaving, the family heard that the man who had built that farmhouse had been murdered there by his hatchet-wielding wife. They also discovered that the new owners of the farm lived in the haunted building for less than a year. They quickly built a new place, on the corner of the land farthest from where the old house stood.

Have you ever been in a building, and not known what's there? I was ready to sell it, or just run away.

Dale Orsted, Proprietor

The Moose Head Inn, Kenosee Lake

September 24, 1994

Mrs. Seymour's Search

ACCORDING TO LOCAL LEGEND, THE WOODEN SHUTTERS ON THE NORTH WALL OF THE OLD SEYMOUR HOUSE OFTEN MOVE WITHOUT THE HELP OF ANY WIND.

In October of 1993, Western People *ran an intriguing story about a haunted house that is now part of the Boy Scouts' Camp Gilwell, near Fort Qu'Appelle. Hazel Jardine, who wrote that original piece, generously shared her research with me.*

It's a two-storey abomination with jaundiced plaster and jutting upstairs windows that keep watch over the land it squats on. This narrow property dividing scenic Mission Lake and the highway between Fort Qu'Appelle and Lebret has something rare; a haunted house that appears dressed to play the part.

It can act the part, too. There are heavy green wooden shutters on the north wall that reportedly bang open and closed when there isn't enough breeze to bring up a ripple on the lake. There are interior lights blazing on occasions when the house is empty and the electrical service box has been deactivated and locked. And, as with any self-respecting haunt, there is a story.

The big yellow house was once owned by Saskatchewan's first minister of health, Dr. Morris Seymour. For many years, he lived there happily with his wife and their two small, beloved dogs.

Aside from his political duties, Dr. Seymour maintained a general practice in Fort Qu'Appelle. The man's devotion to his patients and a lack of proper treatment facilities, early in the century, may have precipitated a tragedy. Mrs. Seymour died at a young age, and it was rumoured to be because her husband had been ministering to infectious tuberculosis patients in their home.

Time passed, and the doctor remarried. Unfortunately, the second Mrs. Seymour wanted nothing to do with the first Mrs. Seymour's two dogs. She insisted they go, and refused to budge on the issue. Dr. Seymour resigned himself to the situation and, not having the heart to put the animals to sleep, found boarding places for them.

As fate would have it the pets outlived their master, who passed away some years later. His widow likely didn't want to be bothered with the expense of the dogs any longer, and had them put down. This must have been too great an offense for the spirit of the first Mrs. Seymour to ignore, for that's when she returned.

At first it was only the sound of slippered footsteps, shuffling across the ceiling of the second wife's downstairs bedroom. In time, the shutters began rattling unexplainably and whistling noises were heard, as the late Mrs. Seymour seemed to be searching for her poor, lost dogs. When the dead woman's apparition was seen walking about the second floor, it was too much for her successor to bear. Bags were packed immediately, and the distressed woman left the house, never to return.

Eventually, the house was donated to the local Boy Scouts' organization, and became part of Camp Gilwell. The kitchen was useful, and the downstairs living room was occasionally needed for meetings on rainy days, but the second floor of the house was virtually abandoned. The story of the restless spirit who once walked those rooms was kept very much alive, thanks to decades of storytelling and the eager imaginations of hundreds of young boys.

One night, in the glow of a flickering campfire, Camp Gilwell's caretaker carefully relayed the tale to a number of nervous Scouts. Eyes grew wider and the tension of the story mounted. Suddenly, one boy jumped up frantically pointing to the bushes beside the house.

"There was a woman!" he cried. "And a little dog behind her! I swear, I saw them just run into the trees!"

THIS MAY HAVE BEEN AN APPEALING PLACE WHEN DOCTOR AND
MRS. SEYMOUR FIRST LIVED IN IT, BUT TODAY IT HAS THE AIR OF
A STEREOTYPICAL HAUNTED HOUSE. INTERESTINGLY, THAT'S WHAT
IT IS REPORTED TO BE.

Everyone turned to look, but no one saw a thing. The boy was probably the object of teasing for the remainder of the evening, and may have regretted his moment of wild imagination. It did, however, get the caretaker thinking.

He was a man who could tell a fabulous ghost story, yet had never believed in ghosts. Consequently, he had never been curious enough to investigate the forgotten upstairs of the old Seymour house. But on this night, as the campfire embers died and the Boy Scouts settled into their tents, he wanted to take a look.

Carrying a powerful flashlight, the caretaker pried open the rain-swollen front door. The shutters banged in protest. Once inside, he shone his light up the old stairwell and, careful not to lean his weight on the rickety bannister, began to ascend. When he reached the top, he froze.

Because the top floor was unused and unattended, there was a layer of dust nearly an inch thick on the floor. As the caretaker stood at the top of the stairs, he could clearly see footsteps in that dust.

They were small footprints, as if made by a woman's slippers. Beside them, apparently following the woman into the bedroom, were the plain tracks of a small dog.

For someone who never believed in ghosts, the caretaker admitted to leaving the Seymour house in a hurry, that night.

In recent years, the Seymour house has been remodelled to better serve the needs at Camp Gilwell. Several walls and the top floor of the house were completely taken out, leaving a large, open-air room. The area that Mrs. Seymour's spirit once haunted is now a vast space, hosting nothing but a ceiling fan. Interestingly, that fan is reported to occasionally switch on and off of its own volition.

They say nobody knows why.

Prince Albert's Cultured Spirits

LATE AT NIGHT, WHEN NO ONE IS IN THE BUILDING, PEOPLE HAVE
REPORTED SEEING FACES AND LIGHTS IN THE SECOND-STOREY AND
ATTIC WINDOWS OF THE PRINCE ALBERT ARTS CENTRE.

The beautiful building that is now the Prince Albert Arts Centre is
actually one of the few nineteenth-century town halls still standing on the
prairies. It was built in 1892-93; two years after the railway arrived in
town and more than ten years before Prince Albert was incorporated as a
city.

The handsome brick structure was designed to serve many purposes.
Within it were meeting rooms, the municipal offices, jail cells and a grand
theatre. After the new city hall was built, it became the Arts Centre, and
perhaps a home to one or two ghosts from its magnificent past.

Every year, the Prince Albert Arts Centre hosts a popular gem show. Ruth Gillingham, the program supervisor who has worked there for over a dozen years, will always remember one of these events in particular – and not because of the dazzling beauty of the stones.

"Due to the value of the displays, this is one time of year when you'll find staff on hand around the clock," Ruth said, explaining how she came to be alone in the Arts Centre late one night. The doors were locked and Ruth had to wait until midnight for a commissionaire to relieve her.

As she quietly worked in the downstairs office, she heard footsteps on the second floor. Ruth thought that some kids had probably hidden themselves at closing time and were planning to spend the night. She climbed the main staircase, expecting to find them in the huge studio that was once Prince Albert's finest theatre. Instead, she found nothing. Attributing the noises to her imagination, Ruth went back down to the office and resumed her paperwork.

Within minutes, she could again hear the distinct sound of people walking around above her head. Quite certain this time that the sounds were not the result of her creative mind, she decided to sneak up the back staircase and surprise her visitors.

"We used to have the looms up there, covering half of the studio area," said Ruth. "We'd always keep them draped, so that if there was any dust, it wouldn't get on the weavings." Ruth suspected that the kids had been hiding under the sheets, so she wasn't fooled a second time when she found a seemingly empty room.

To avoid having to uncover each of the looms individually, Ruth decided to use a little trickery to flush the intruders out. "I made a big business out of jingling my keys," she said, "and said to myself in a loud voice, 'Well, obviously there's no one here ... might as well lock up and go home.'" She then turned out all the lights in the building and went back to the office to silently wait and watch.

The Prince Albert Arts Centre boasts one of those stately wooden staircases that, over many years, has become as noisy as it is elegant. Ruth was sure that once the kids felt the building was empty, they would come downstairs to snoop around, and so she sat in the dark-ened office facing the staircase, waiting for the familiar creaking sounds. She didn't have to wait long.

There it was – the complaining groan of each wooden step, as someone began to descend. Ruth was excited, thinking her plan worked, but the excitement soon turned to confusion. Although the staircase was in plain view, and the footsteps had nearly reached the bottom, there was no one there. Ruth wasted no time gathering her purse and car keys and left the office.

"I was out waiting by the front door for the commissionaire to arrive," she said, "because that was my first real experience with it and I was a little uneasy."

Although Ruth didn't immediately tell anyone of her experience, she soon learned that there had been other strange incidents. People on the street had claimed to see faces in the attic window, lights blazing, and groups of people milling around on the second floor. All this was reported at two or three in the morning, when even the janitor was long gone. Some of this could have been attributed to the fact that any century-old building invites such stories, but there were more credible accounts from the staff.

"People have heard music playing, upstairs," Ruth explained. "Ballroom music, dancing music, that kind of thing ... and that's after the building's been closed and locked for the night." There had also been a number of strange happenings in the basement, which was once the city's jail. The walls were whitewashed mud and clay, four to six feet thick, and there were no opening windows; yet unexplainably, doors would shut by themselves, and cold breezes appeared out of nowhere.

For a while, the Arts Centre had an unofficial mascot, a dog who frequently came to work with his mistress. "Boots" seemed to sense something odd in the basement, and late one evening, became absolutely frantic as Ruth worked down there in the mud room. He stood in the doorway, yelping insanely, and would not budge. Ruth had to literally climb over the dog to see what was in the hallway, upsetting him so. The area outside the mud room seemed unusually cold, but Ruth found nothing else that night to explain the little mascot's bizarre behavior.

At some point, Ruth shared that story with a British woman who had begun working at the Arts Centre. The woman, who had a reputation as a sensitive, casually remarked that it must have been the ghosts that upset the dog. Ruth, fearing ridicule, had never told anyone of her experiences in the building, and she warily asked the woman what she meant.

"Oh come now!" the woman asserted. "You've worked here for years, don't tell me you don't know about the ghosts!"

"She told me that there were two ghosts in the building," said Ruth. "A young lady and a middle-aged man; two lost souls. That's how she explained it to me." Since then, Ruth claims she has never been afraid of the spirits. As she puts it, "they've never harmed anyone or done anything malicious, so you live with it. What can you do?"

Apparently one thing you can do is promote it. On Hallowe'en, the Arts Centre takes its ghosts public, and children are encouraged to remember them in their arts and crafts. Instead of being afraid of what they don't understand, the kids have been known to make hand-print posters with paint, leaving room on the paper for a few "ghostly" prints, as well.

Recently, the otherworldly inhabitants of the Arts Centre had to deal with the disruption of some minor renovations. There are many reports of spirits reacting negatively to such changes in their environment, and this was no exception. The "acting up" was minor, though, and Ruth feels she knows why.

"The building is a historic landmark, so we were trying very hard to maintain the original design and appearance." She theorizes that because there were few major changes to the one-hundred-year-old structure, the ghosts had little reason to get upset. When they do get troublesome, however, the staff now knows how to deal with them.

"You just talk to them," Ruth explains, "say, 'oh, come on, quit fooling around.'"

It's a simple solution that seems to work, because, as Ruth says, "no one's ever left here screaming." She pauses, and adds thoughtfully, "that I know of, anyway."

If there's such a thing as a secure home in the afterlife, these particular souls have it. Since the Prince Albert Arts Centre has been declared a historic landmark, it will be maintained forever and its music-loving spirits will never face the threat of having their haunt torn down.

The Legend of the Valley

An Azure river cuts through rolling hills in Saskatchewan's Qu'Appelle Valley. The area owes its name to a native Indian legend.

One of Saskatchewan's most beautiful attractions is the scenic Qu'Appelle Valley, stretching east to west across nearly two-thirds of the province. Created in ancient times as a glacial spillway, it now serves as a home to lakes, parks, campgrounds, resort villages and picturesque communities.

The valley's name comes from a bittersweet Native Indian legend replete with supernatural overtones.

While the Qu'Appelle Valley is renowned for its natural beauty, the first white settlers chose it for its natural convenience. The valley offered a central location and handy gateway to the north for early fur traders, and by 1804, the North West Company had moved in.

David Harmon was one of those first traders. When he arrived, local Cree Indians told him the story behind the name Kahtapwao, or "What is Calling." As the North West Company conducted business in French, the name was eventually translated to Qu'Appelle, meaning, in English, "Who Calls?"

The legend is that of a young Indian brave, making a long journey home to see his betrothed, a beautiful Indian maiden. So eager was he to see her, he paddled his canoe day and night, ignoring hunger and fatigue in favour of haste.

Finally, one evening, he joyously realized that he was within a day of seeing his true love. Fantasizing about the approaching reunion, he rested for a moment, letting the current gently move him downstream. Suddenly, from the shadows of the shore, the brave heard a voice tenderly call his name.

"Who calls?" the brave cried out, and strained to listen for an answer.

Again, above the whispering night wind, he heard his name.

More urgently, he pleaded, "Who calls?" His answer was the lonely echo of his own frightened voice, as the pale moon rose in the east.

Worried that the voice had been an omen of tragedy, the young brave hurried on to his destination. When he arrived, his worst fears were confirmed. Death-fires had been lit along the shore, and the mournful wails of the people could be heard for a mile. Before the brave stepped out of his canoe, he knew his maiden had died.

He was taken to see her, and as he stood there in anguish, an old woman tried to console him.

"She called for you twice, last night," said the woman.

Shaken, the brave asked when.

"As the moon was rising, just before she passed away."

According to E. Pauline Johnson's wonderful poem, *The Legend of the Qu'Appelle Valley*, to this day, "when the moonrise tips the distant hill," the dying young maiden's haunting voice can be heard on the wind. It is she "who calls" her lover to her deathbed, in a tragic tale that named the beautiful valley.

A version of the original Cree word, "Kahtapwao" has since been used in the names of Katepwa Beach, a recreational area, and Katepwa Point Provincial Park.

If you're a person who believes in spirits, you're not going to chalk up
something automatically to coincidence. You're going to think about
it. [As a believer], your mind's a little more open.

Ruth Gillingham,
Program Supervisor
The Prince Albert Arts Centre
September 19, 1994

A Picture-Perfect Home

The popular notion is that all spirits tend to be attached to a certain location, and will remain no matter what physical changes take place there. In fact, there are a number of stories involving ghosts who pack up and leave; to follow a person, an object, even building materials. A pretty young teacher named Candy Fay shared this story of an entire house that was moved, along with its otherworldly inhabitants.

"Oh, it was a beautiful house," Candy told me one day, on the phone. "It had turrets and even a widow's walk. It was really something to see."

It's no wonder, then, that the Bennet family (a pseudonym) felt they were getting a rare deal when they bought their lovely old place for a mere thousand dollars. It was the early seventies, and the elegant Saskatoon neighbourhood that the house was part of had been slated for redevelopment. A number of dramatic, turn-of-the-century structures were available for a song, provided the buyers were willing to move them. The Bennets put out another few hundred dollars to relocate the building to their acreage, and became the proud owners of a charming "character" home.

A bit of painting was done, a few repairs taken care of, and the Bennets were soon living in their seventy-year-old bargain. The house felt cozy and comfortable from the beginning, but it wasn't long before some unusual occurrences were concerning the family.

Footsteps were frequently heard on the staircase, and in the upstairs hall, leading into one particular bedroom. Occasionally, someone would catch a whiff of strong perfume, and there would be no explanation. Although all old houses admit the odd breeze, the family noticed that this one seemed to have more than its share of cold spots, and not necessarily near the doors and windows. Things frequently went missing, as well, and would show up in different and unusual locations.

The Bennet's twelve-year-old son slept in the upstairs bedroom where the phantom footsteps were frequently heard. One night, he awoke to find a woman standing beside the bed, peering down at him.

She wasn't a threatening presence, but certainly an unsettling one, in her Victorian attire. If the Bennets had been hesitant to admit they were sharing their home with something spectral, this startling incident would have made it impossible to deny.

One day shortly thereafter, Mrs. Bennet was sorting through some things in the attic. She was surprised to discover some items that must have belonged to a previous owner. They had been stashed away so well, they were moved with the house, unnoticed.

The most interesting find was a pair of framed portraits; a man and a woman, in old-fashioned clothing and hairstyles. Mrs. Bennet thought the photographs, in their antique frames, would be a marvelous complement to the decor of the house. She dusted them off, and hung them in the downstairs hall, at the foot of the staircase.

And that's when it stopped.

The footsteps, the perfume, the missing objects; they all came to an end. No matter what the weather was outside, there were no more unreasonably cold spots in the house. There were no more apparitions, no more ghostly activity of *any* kind from the moment the portraits were hung.

"Now, you have to understand," Candy said, "Mrs. Bennet was intelligent, aggressive, and one of the toughest women I ever met. She was a no-nonsense person; definitely not the type to submit to hysterical delusions. But for the entire time I knew her, she refused to let anyone even *touch* those pictures."

And apparently, wisely so. It must have put the spirits at peace to have a place of honour in their old home, because in addition to being free from paranormal activity, Candy describes the house as being particularly welcoming and warm. She would know, having spent a great deal of time there as a family friend of the Bennets. There was one night she even spent alone, house-sitting. I asked if anything at all disturbed her.

"Oh no," she laughed, then admitted, "I did have a little trouble getting to sleep, because of all the stories, but nothing happened."

So it was true then, that nothing unusual ever happened, after the portraits were hung?

"Well, there was one thing," Candy added. "I don't know if it was the old style of colourizing the photos, or maybe something more supernatural, but no matter where you were in the downstairs hall ... the people in the picture ... their eyes seemed to be looking right at you."

Just your average ghostly couple, keeping a careful watch over their home.

Uncle Ben's House

BEN ECKERT ONCE OWNED THIS HOUSE, IN THE PEACEFUL TOWN OF CARLYLE. HIS NIECE, DEENA, WAS ONE OF SEVERAL FAMILY MEMBERS WHO EXPERIENCED STRANGE EVENTS THERE.

Popular horror fiction abounds with stories of "the bad place." Dracula's castle; Stephen King's Overlook Hotel in The Shining*; Shirley Jackson's infamous "Hill House." But does such a thing exist in real life? Are there buildings that have "soured"; places that exude negativity along with a few traditional ghosts? Vancouver artisan Deena Gusul might think so.*

The way Deena talks, there's very little doubt that Ben Eckert must have been her favourite uncle.

"He held a lot of importance to a lot of people," she said reverently, adding that Ben was particularly popular with the younger family members. "When I was twelve, I could relate to him. He was always understanding, and really 'with it.'"

Ben was indeed beloved by his relatives. People may have assumed, then, that when Ben passed away, his family would be reluctant to part with the home he had lived in for so many of his years. On the contrary, it was sold as quickly as possible, because of what Deena could only describe as "bad associations."

"Does that sound irrational?" she asked. Probably not to the many family members who took advantage over the years of Ben's generous open-door policy. For it was common to experience things that were unexplainable, while enjoying their uncle's hospitality.

Deena recalled that as a child she heard all kinds of stories about the unassuming bungalow that her great-uncle Ben owned in Carlyle, Saskatchewan. Over time, she forgot the details, but retained that there was a sense of spookiness about them. It seemed that almost everyone in the family could relay these tales, but at the same time, they strove to trivialize them.

"I think it was because we didn't want to believe them," she told me. "We all stayed there at one point or another."

Indeed, Ben's welcome mat was always out and he gladly received people, often for extended stays. One of Deena's cousins virtually grew up in his house. After moving away, however, she would come home to see Ben, but never, under any circumstances, stay overnight. No explanation was ever offered.

Deena's mother, once visiting Ben, was quite traumatized when she received a visitor of her own: the apparition of her late sister. While the spirit spoke to her, she felt helpless; completely immobilized. The incident proved so distressing that she has never shared further details of it, or told anyone what her sister had to say.

Deena herself experienced graphic nightmares, whenever she slept in one particular bedroom. The only time she ever sleepwalked was at Ben's, and in her unconscious state she actually left the house. Perhaps at some psychic level, she felt it was best to leave.

The most memorable event for Deena, however, happened back in 1979. She was twelve years old, and living in Carlyle with a great-aunt (Ben Eckert's sister). Deena and her sister, Darcy, would often stop by Ben's house after school, and on this particular day, Deena was more excited about the visit than usual. The reason was that there were new kittens to play with; any twelve-year-old girl's idea of ultimate fun. Deena arrived at the house first, and let herself in. "It was small-town Saskatchewan," she explained, "No one locked their doors." She assumed that Darcy, who was older and attended a different school, would be along shortly.

Sure enough, as Deena began to play with the tiny kittens in the living room, she heard a young girl's voice in the back porch. The girl was cooing affectionately, as if talking to the kittens, but all of the kittens were with Deena. More specifically, they were scrambling to a cowering position beneath the safety of a heavy buffet, apparently terrified of the mewing voice. "Very un-cat-like behavior," Deena notes, today.

Thinking it must be Darcy, Deena followed the sound of the voice to the back porch. When she arrived, however, she was greeted with heavy silence and an empty room. The door was securely shut, and there was no sign of anyone having come in. Deena remembers having an overwhelming sense of discomfort.

Showing enormous courage, Deena searched the porch thoroughly and even gave the basement a cursory glance before returning to the living room. Unsettled and nervous, she decided to phone her aunt.

Deena dialed the number from memory and connected with a busy signal. She hung up, waited uneasily for a couple of minutes, and tried again. Busy. Six times, she carefully dialed, and six times, Deena heard the same flat buzz. Finally, on the seventh attempt, her aunt picked up the phone. "Who've you been talking to?" asked Deena. "I've been trying to get through for ten minutes!" There was a confused silence before Deena's aunt replied.

"This is the first time the phone's rung, this afternoon."

Deena's aunt also revealed that Darcy was at her house, and had gone there directly after school. That dispelled any notion Deena had that her older sister was perhaps playing a trick on her. She hung up the phone and left Ben's house immediately.

Years later, Deena still has no explanation for the events of that afternoon. She is still sure she dialed the number correctly, she still knows that she heard the voice, and she still remembers the terrified reaction of the kittens. The only addition to the story came recently, when Deena had a chance to visit with Darcy at a family wedding. The conversation turned to Ben and his house, and Deena decided to tell her sister about her strange experience there.

As Deena carefully described the strange quality of the voice, Darcy blanched. "Oh my god!" she exclaimed, then told Deena she knew the voice.

How?

"That exact thing happened to me," Darcy confessed. "But I never told you. I never told anyone."

It makes one wonder how many other unexplainable experiences Ben Eckert's relatives have shared, in the modest little house in Carlyle.

There is no certain reason why Ben Eckert's house would have been such a centre for paranormal activity, but according to Deena, the family shared a theory. It seems that when the house was built, circa 1930, quite a bit of scrap lumber that had been salvaged from an ancient barn was used.

"The rumour is," said Deena, "that something terrible happened in that barn."

Perhaps the negative energy of that event travelled with the very materials used to build the house.

The Curse of the Mckees

A BITTER EPITAPH MARKS THE GRAVES OF THREE MINERS KILLED IN THE "BLACK TUESDAY" RIOT. ANDY MCKEE'S MOTHER AND GRAND-FATHER REST IN THIS SMALL CEMETERY — EITHER IN UNMARKED GRAVES, OR BENEATH WEATHERED MARKERS WITH NAMES AND DATES LONG WORN AWAY.

The Riel Rebellion. The Great Depression. It is impossible to grow up on Saskatchewan soil and not hear stories of these history-shaping times.

It's interesting to note that one of the province's most intriguing super-natural tales takes place against the backdrop of both these momentous events, and the forty-five years spanning between. This is the story of the Mckee family; three generations of men bound by the murderous actions of one.

Andy Mckee had no fond memories of his grandfather, but he would admit that the man could tell a story. And when Andy was growing up lonely and bored, on an isolated, drought-ravaged farm east of Bienfait, that must have been a quality to appreciate.

59

When Grandfather Mckee was in a rare amicable mood, he would fire Andy's imagination with colorful accounts of the famous buffalo hunts. His vivid descriptions belied the fact that by the time he had seen the prairies, the buffalo had been hunted nearly to extinction. Andy enjoyed the stories anyway.

Grandfather's repertoire of tall tales also included stories of the Northwest Rebellion, and Andy knew these had at least some basis in fact. The elder Mckee had come west to help fight down Riel's uprising. With each retelling of his adventure, however, the number of Métis he boasted of having killed grew larger.

In Val Clery's book, *Ghost Stories of Canada* (1985), Andy Mckee describes his grandfather as "a cantankerous, wicked old bastard" who dismissed the Métis people as "stinking heathens" and, revealing his Orangeman nature, "dirty papists." Indeed, the old man may have had few endearing qualities, but his racism simply identified him as a product of his time.

In 1885, when Mckee came west with the militia, violent anti-Indian sentiment had reached its peak. In the April 23, 1885 edition of the *Saskatchewan Herald*, one article laments the news that "Nearly a score of our citizens have been slain without a moment's warning by ingrates whose interests they guarded as carefully as they did their own, and whose hands were daily opened in charity to the men they looked upon as unfortunate and to be pitied." Evidently, the Métis people's legitimate land claims were not among the aforementioned guarded interests.

A few inches away, on the same newspaper page, it is concluded that "this gives weight to the old adage that the only good Indians are the dead ones."

It was in this climate of hatred that Mckee met the west, and he lowered himself to the occasion admirably. Following the rebellion, he took out a homestead claim on the farm near Bienfait. When he discovered a Métis family stubbornly squatting by the Souris River on his land, he employed a swift, pragmatic solution. He shot them all, and buried the bodies where they fell. It may have been that nobody knew what happened on the isolated farm, or it may have been that nobody cared. Whatever the reason, no form of earthly justice was ever meted out for the crime.

Mckee's new life on the prairies did not prove to be an easy one. He married and had a son, but his wife died soon after the boy's birth. The land itself seemed turned against him, with year after dry year, when the topsoil simply blew away, and seasons of horrible blight, when it didn't. Eventually his son married, and in 1916, Andy was born, but barely a year later the young mother died in childbirth. A newborn daughter also perished. This tragedy left three generations of Mckee men to fend for themselves.

Andy's father worked in the nearby coal mines from August through March, and farmed the family's stubborn quarter-section the rest of the year. Economic necessity had him toiling long hours, no matter what the season; as a result, Andy was raised primarily by his grandfather.

It was a bleak existence for a boy, worsened by the fact of his grandfather's personality. And, as if Andy's poverty-beset rural life wasn't restrictive enough, the old man had a rigid rule that even limited the boy's harmless daytime wanderings: he was never to set foot on the "bottom land," near the river.

The Mckee farm was divided into two sections by a bluff; a sharp drop of one hundred feet that led to the valley of the Souris River. The soil down there was a little richer, and tended not to dry out as badly. The Mckees might have fared better as farmers, had they worked the bottom land, but the old man expressly forbade it. To ensure that his warning was heeded, he threatened that should they ever disregard his wishes, he would banish his son from the farm and give Andy the beating of his life. For years, everyone kept to the high ground, and confrontation on the issue was avoided.

In 1930, farmers in the Bienfait area were feeling the harsh sting of the Depression. Andy's father was forced to spend more hours working for less and, in a reversal of roles, fourteen-year-old Andy began caring for his failing grandfather.

Perhaps the increasing dreariness of his life called for some adventure, perhaps it was easier to disobey a feeble old man in his seventies, or perhaps it was the rebellion of adolescence; but Andy decided one day to explore the bottom land.

There was a gully where he knew he could climb down the cliff, and Andy's heart was beating with excitement as he approached it. It was a hot, dry, August day, and the thought of sitting on the forbidden river bank and splashing his bare feet in the Souris held great appeal. Andy had taken fewer than a half-dozen steps down the hill, however, when he was overcome with dread. It wasn't fear of his grandfather; the old man could no longer walk as far as the bluff. It was a sense that this was a bad place, a poisoned place, and Andy no longer wanted his summer afternoon adventure.

The awful feeling refused to leave him, yet Andy felt compelled to finish his journey. He was sweating from the fear, more than the heat, by the time he reached the river. Terribly, unexplainably upset, he began to shiver and weep, as he walked back toward the gully.

In the shadows that bled from the bottom of the cliff, Andy saw him; a tall, dark man with piercing eyes. He wore a wide-brimmed hat and a fringed buckskin jacket, and as Andy stared in shock, the man raised his arm and pointed accusingly. He was pointing at Andy.

Suddenly, the boy was surrounded with loud, echoing sounds, and held the certain knowledge that if he stayed, he would die. He scrambled up the side of the hill, praying desperately that he would reach safety before whatever lived in the bottom land could reach him.

He made it – and on shaky legs, returned to the house. Andy never looked behind him, and vowed he would never set foot on the bottom land again. Having had enough trouble for the day, he didn't even mention the incident to his grandfather.

Andy made dinner for them both, then went to bed early as the elder Mckee sat at the kitchen table poring over his Bible. What followed was the worst nightmare of Andy's young life, a heart-stopping experience he described to Val Clery:

> Terrifying though that day had been for me,
> the night was a thousand times worse. Immediately
> I was lost in a nightmare. I could see myself
> lying down at the foot of this bluff. It was
> dark, and the darkness was full of bellowing
> animals and shouts and guns being fired. I
> couldn't move and I was splattered with dung
> and blood. All around me great hairy bodies
> were thudding down and I was certain that I was
> going to be crushed and buried. It was what my
> granddad had told me about so often, the buffalo
> run. And I was going to be killed.

Andy awoke drenched with sweat, his throat parched from screaming. He must have wondered why he hadn't woken his grandfather, but when the boy ventured to the kitchen for a dipper of water, it became obvious.

Andy's grandfather was dead. The flickering lamplight showed him still propped in the kitchen chair, his head resting on the Bible and his eyes staring vacantly ahead. One generation of the Mckee men was gone.

It took every penny that Andy's father had to give the old man a decent burial. And as the Depression raged on, that little bit of security cash was impossible to replace.

Nineteen thirty-one was the Mckee's most devastating year. Little snow in the winter and no rain through the spring and summer rendered their dusty farm unable to produce even enough vegetables to feed the two of them. Often, there was no gas for the truck, and therefore, no way to take advantage of free food and clothing brought to Bienfait on occasional relief trains from the east. And at the coal mines, which had always been a reliable, if back-breaking, source of income, serious labour trouble was brewing.

The crushing conditions of the Great Depression put both miners and mine operators under debilitating economic pressure. Top market prices for lignite, a soft coal, had dropped by more than 25 percent, and wages fell as a result. Men were working up to sixteen hours a day, and claimed they were not getting true weights for the coal they mined. Worse, what little money they were making did not seem to be truly theirs, as they were forced to deal with company stores. The situation volatized, and by September 7, 1931, every mining company in the Estevan-Bienfait area, except the Truax-Traer Co., was on strike.

Both sides were unyielding; and as numerous conciliatory efforts failed, mine operators urged the Saskatchewan government to provide ample police protection for their property and equipment. As hostilities grew, so did the ranks of the RCMP in Estevan. On September 29, the day of a planned labour demonstration, there were at least eighty-five red serge uniforms lined up along Fourth Street.

Andy's father felt it was important to stand with his fellow workers, so on the day of the demonstration, he walked all the way into Bienfait to catch a ride. It was shortly after noon when they assembled, some 400 miners and their families, to begin their fateful march into Estevan.

That morning, Estevan's town council had passed a resolution refusing to grant a parade permit, but it was a useless gesture in the face of the miners' determination. They marched on, peacefully, until the Estevan chief of police approached, ordering them to leave town.

There was a heated exchange of words, and a single violent gesture that started the melee. For forty-five minutes, the miners and police clashed in a bloody riot that was to claim three young lives and stain the history books. It was September 29, 1931; from that point forward, known as "Black Tuesday."

Mckee managed to dodge the bullets and rocks. He avoided arrest and walked over twenty-five exhausting miles back to the farm. But when he got there, Andy could see that he was a broken man. There was surely no hope for decent employment now, and the Mckee's very survival was at stake.

The next day, as Saskatchewan newspapers devoted their front pages to listing the injured and the dead, Andy's father made a decision. He told his son that if they didn't want to freeze to death that winter, they'd have to "gopher out some coal." It was common practice in the area for people to dig small holes along a seam of coal, and help themselves to what they found. Andy's dad had been mining long enough to know where the coal was on his land; it ran along the river bank, in the bottom land.

Andy begged his father not to do it, insisting that the old man had been right; it was a bad place, a haunted place. His father just laughed, and called it Irish superstition. Since the elder Mckee was dead, and no longer able to kick them off the land, he was going to do what was necessary. He gathered his pick and shovel, and asked once more whether Andy was going to help him. Andy shook his head, and helplessly watched as his father walked down over the bluff.

It was the last time Andy would see him alive.

The boy waited for what seemed to be an eternity, but his father didn't come home. Finally, at dusk, Andy headed for the gully that he knew would take him down to the river bed.

The shadows were darkening by the minute. Andy called for his dad again and again, but received no answer. Truly, he didn't expect one. He knew what had been down there, waiting for his father in the bottom land.

Strangely enough, Andy felt no fear as he began to descend the bluff. As he said in Clery's book, he was certain of what he'd find.

> The bushes right below here were crushed flat.
> My dad's body hardly looked human, it was so
> crushed and broken and torn. There was no face
> left. And the smell ... it was what I'd smelled in
> my nightmare – blood and dung and the hot bodies
> of animals ...

The pick and shovel lay on the ground. They'd touched no coal in the river bank, that day; instead, Andy Mckee used them to bury the remains of his father in the bottom land.

When he finished the sombre chore and looked up, he saw the tall figure of the Métis man watching from the shadows. Andy felt no fear, though. His grandfather had murdered the Métis family, but his father, trampled under the hooves of a thousand ghostly bison, had paid the debt.

Andy tossed the tools into the bushes, and walked back up to the top of the gully. He didn't stop there to reflect, but kept walking. He didn't stop at the house, but kept walking. Andy walked most of the night, until he reached Estevan. There, he jumped a freight train to Toronto; leaving behind, forever, his cursed existence on the dusty southeastern Saskatchewan farm.

The three miners who were slain by police bullets were later interred in the Bienfait cemetery. A procession of 600 men, women and children followed the caskets; the service was delivered with great solemnity and the hymns were heartfelt.

Andy Mckee's father had considered himself lucky not be killed on Black Tuesday. How ironic that his fate was to be unceremoniously and anonymously buried on his own land, before the very funeral of those three men whom he pitied.

He, too, was a victim, but one destined never to be mentioned in the history books.

Toddler Haunts Duplex

ACCORDING TO PREVIOUS TENANTS, THIS MODEST SASKATOON
DUPLEX IS HAUNTED BY THE GHOST OF A CHILD.

It is believed that many spirits remain trapped on the physical plane because they have died too suddenly. This would explain the presence that occupies the basement of a duplex on a quiet Saskatoon crescent.

If Debbie had not been such a particular housekeeper, it might have taken her longer to realize that the basement suite she moved into was haunted. But in her own words, "Everything has its place" in Debbie's house, so when things were frequently *out* of place, she noticed.

"When I first moved in, I hardly spent any time there," Debbie admits. But it seemed that every day, when she returned to her apartment, something was out of order. Once, after being away for a weekend, Debbie came home to a frustratingly large mess. Cassette tapes that had been carefully filed were randomly mixed, all the lights in the house had been unplugged, and there was sticky juice spilled on the kitchen floor. Irritated, she asked her upstairs neighbours and friends, Gary and Lori, about the incident. "Not to be rude," Debbie said, "but do you let your kids play down here, when I'm gone?" They looked at each other blankly, confused by the question. It seems Debbie had the only key.

When Debbie began spending more time in the apartment, strange things began to happen right before her eyes. Lights would switch on and off by themselves. The television would come on in the middle of the night. A hot-water tap that could only be turned on with pliers would start running on its own. And every time Debbie would sit down to read, she'd feel someone's icy breath on her shoulder. After awhile, she dreaded going home, because she never knew what was going to happen.

Lori and Gary were beginning to notice some out-of-the-ordinary occurrences, as well. There would be audible footsteps and water running in the basement suite when they knew Debbie wasn't home. And one night, they switched off the television and lights at about one o'clock, before retiring. Just as they were drifting off to sleep, however, they were startled by noises in the living room. Gary went out there, expecting to confront a burglar, and found the TV had been turned back on.

One night, after witnessing a flurry of paranormal activity, the three friends desperately appealed to the police for help. The only assistance found there was a suggestion to call a priest. "We never did," said Lori, acknowledging the difficulty of finding reputable help, in that situation. "I mean, who are you going to call? 'Ghostbusters?'"

Because of the mischievous nature of many of the incidents, Debbie had always had a hunch the ghost was a child. One afternoon, frustrated with the flashing lights and cold spots in her apartment, she went upstairs to share her theory. "Was there ever a child who died in this place?" she asked. "I just feel that it's a little kid who's stuck between here and there." Gary and Lori had a friend sitting at the kitchen table that day. He suddenly went white. It turned out that the man's two-year-old niece had been struck and killed by a car in front of the duplex, years before. The toddler's family had lived in the basement suite that Debbie now occupied.

Somewhat bolstered by the knowledge, Debbie went downstairs to talk to the ghost. "Don't do this to me," she demanded. "I know who you are, and I'm not afraid of you." The apartment was calmer for a short period after that. The truth was, though, that Debbie was still quite afraid. She found it difficult to be brave for her twelve-year-old daughter, when inside, she herself was terrified of the force that occupied her home.

Debbie wasn't the only person who sensed that this could be a very negative and frightening entity. She has relatives who are native and, according to Debbie, more sensitive in spiritual matters. Many of them wouldn't set foot in her home. One uncle mustered the courage to visit twice, then firmly refused to return. He later confided in Debbie that he felt distinctly unwelcome by the spirit.

"There were the smells, too," said Debbie. "Sudden scents of either lilac or burnt toast. They were so strong, they could make me nauseous." There were no lilac trees close to the duplex, and Debbie never wore perfume. As for the burnt toast, the last time she smelled it was just before she moved, and her toaster had been packed away for three days. Could it have been from upstairs? Not likely. "Lori and Gary were away," Debbie explained.

Debbie was able to explain away those smells, for awhile. She was pregnant while she lived in the duplex, and thought that perhaps they were some sort of odd symptom. That was later disproved, but while her pregnancy didn't "cause" the perception of the smells, it did seem to affect the amount of paranormal activity that happened. It increased steadily, as her pregnancy progressed.

Debbie was facing a difficult personal decision, with this pregnancy. She was in the process of a divorce, and her soon-to-be ex-husband was the father of the child. She had a promising future with a wonderful new man she had met, but wondered how he would accept the baby. She considered giving it up for adoption, to give everyone a clean start, but it was a wrenching decision.

Debbie had, earlier in life, given a baby to adoptive parents, and she always kept a picture of this newborn infant on the wall. While she struggled with her problem, the baby's picture kept falling off the wall. Stubbornly, Debbie kept putting it back up, each time with a more formidable nail. "Pretty soon," she said, "I was using a spike to keep it up there." But the picture continued to fall. Eventually, Debbie chose to keep her baby, no matter what the consequences. From that point on, the other child's photo stayed put "with a thumb-tack."

Once the baby was born, Debbie always had the sensation of being watched. The spirit seemed to be fascinated with the baby, too, and paid a great deal of attention to it. The automatic swing Debbie had for her newborn would switch on and off, by itself. And Debbie swears that her baby could "see" the presence that was invisible to her. The infant would "coo" and "talk" continuously, when by herself. When Debbie held her daughter, and tried to get her attention, the child always seemed to be focusing on something just behind her mother's left shoulder. After they left the duplex, however, the baby would always make eye contact.

It was one particularly disturbing incident that cemented Debbie's decision to move. She was in the living room, one day, while her baby napped in the bedroom. Suddenly, there was a loud, continuous banging noise, and Debbie ran to investigate. What she saw will stay with her forever.

The big teddy bear that she'd put in bed with her daughter was being slammed repeatedly against the side of the crib. The baby's fingers were curled around the stuffed animal's foot, but she could hardly be held responsible. She was only two weeks old at the time; an infant with neither the strength nor physical skills to commit such an act.

Debbie knew then that for the safety of her baby and her older daughter, she had to leave the duplex. "Things really started acting up, then," she said. Every time Debbie would begin packing, she'd be overwhelmed by a feeling of suffocation, and be forced to stop. She felt that the ghost had become furious over their leaving. Once she started to move furniture out of the suite, Debbie refused to sleep there at night, fearing the spirit would be angry enough to kill the baby.

On the first night in her new home, however, there was another scare. "I could see these flashing lights, and I was going, 'Oh no! Not again!'" Happily, the phenomenon was caused by nothing more ghostly than a flashlight with a short in its wiring.

Lori and Gary chose to move out of the duplex at the same time. Now, Debbie is happily remarried, and both couples remain close friends and live within a short walk of each other and the duplex they used to share.

"They've gone through a lot of tenants, since we left," observes Debbie, and adds that she still has to walk past her old home, occasionally.

How does it make her feel?

"It gives me the creeps."

An understatement, if ever there was one.

[Paranormal activity] doesn't have to be ominous stuff, you know, for it to be mind-blowing and unsettling. It can be playful, but it's scary if you don't know what's coming next.

It terrorizes some people. Others can take it in stride.

Dr. Buddy Wynn, Parapsychologist
University of Regina
September 26, 1994

A Spirit Solves the Case

The year was 1890 when, in Baltimore, Maryland, a man named William Fuld invented something called the "Ouija" board. For being nothing more than a flat surface painted with letters, numbers, and the words "yes" and "no," it has enjoyed the publicity of tremendous controversy over the years. Psychologists attribute meaningful Ouija messages to trickery or unconscious responses. Parapsychologists believe the game sets favourable conditions for the occurence of extrasensory perception. Spiritualists maintain that it is a way to communicate with the dead. There are strong arguments for each case, but this story, revealed on a radio call-in program, makes it hard to accept the Ouija as simply an innocent Victorian parlour game.

THIS MASS GRAVE IN THE SHELL LAKE CEMETERY HOLDS THE NINE SLAIN MEMBERS OF THE PETERSON FAMILY. EIGHT COFFINS WERE USED; BABY LARRY WAS LAID TO REST WITH HIS MOTHER.

"I have a story regarding a Ouija board, if you have a second to listen to it."

It was a summer afternoon radio talk show. The subject of the day was ghost stories, and the calls had been steady. The man on the telephone offering this story seemed polite and articulate, and the announcer invited him to elaborate. "Many years ago, when my wife was a teenager ..." he began ...

Many years ago turned out to be 1967. It was known as "The Summer of Love" to many, but to the residents of Shell Lake, it would be forever remembered for the senseless and tragic slaughter of a local farm family.

Nine members of the Peterson family were murdered in their own home, in cold blood, when a young man who said he had been "seeing the devil" since he was ten years old went on a grisly rampage with a rifle.

The horror of such a crime in this tiny community of fewer than 300 souls made headlines around the world. In neighbouring areas, men with loaded shotguns stood watch over their families, while the Spiritwood RCMP conducted a gruelling four-day door-to-door search. A few miles away, in another tiny town called Parkside, a group of teenagers were, in a sense, conducting a search of their own.

It was a warm, August evening and, for something interesting to do, the teens had pulled out a Ouija board. They asked it a variety of routine questions, then, decided to inquire about the Peterson case.

"Do you know who the murderer is?" was the first question asked. After a brief pause, the Ouija board answered, "yes."

"Can you give us the murderer's initials?"

The planchette on the board replied by pointing out the letters "V," and "H."

"Will they be caught?"

After a pause, the answer came, "yes."

The spirit must have been reluctant to offer any more direct information, because the group then tried less obvious methods of determining the killer's full identity.

"Is this person in our telephone area?" they asked, and the board answered in the affirmative. A quick scan of the white pages revealed no further clues, however.

Frustrated, they settled on one final question.

"Will any of us ever meet this person?"

The Ouija quickly answered "yes," and then indicated the initials "S.G." Everyone took it to mean Susan Green (a pseudonym), one of the members of the group.

THE BATTLEFORD COURTHOUSE WHERE VICTOR HOFFMAN WAS
TRIED FOR MURDER. AT THE BOTTOM OF THESE STAIRS, A YOUNG
WOMAN FULFILLED A OUIJA BOARD PROPHESY WHEN SHE STARED
DIRECTLY INTO THE KILLER'S EYES.

A couple of days later, on August 19th, the RCMP apprehended the man who would eventually be tried in the Peterson case. His name: Victor Hoffman. "V.H."

Victor lived with his family on a farm by Leask. Not in the Parkside telephone listings, where the teens had looked for him, but certainly in the same telephone book.

All that remained was the Ouija's prophecy regarding young Susan Green. She had never before met Victor Hoffman, and given the circumstances, probably never intended to. But the following January, as police were escorting Victor out of the courthouse in Battleford, Susan happened to be on the street, passing by. At the bottom of the steps, Hoffman dropped something. The police stopped, allowing him to retrieve it. He straightened up, just as Susan Green walked in front of him – and looked directly into her eyes.

"From that minute on, my wife has never, ever played the Ouija board," finished the caller.

"This wasn't a coincidence in your mind?" asked the host of the radio show.

"No, it wasn't. It wasn't." The caller assured hastily. Although he had mentioned being uncomfortable with the idea of Ouija boards, he seemed to have no doubt about the validity of his wife's story.

Could the incident be explained away as coincidence? Is there a chance that ESP (extrasensory perception) played a part? What about spiritual intervention? Is it a possibility that one or more of the Peterson clan, not yet in their graves, tried to identify the man who claimed their lives?

There's no way of knowing, unless, of course, you ask Ouija.

Strange Sights on Sinnet Road

In 1905, a small Catholic community sprouted just east of Lanigan, Saskatchewan. It was named "Sinnet." The nearby service road became known, logically, as "Sinnet Road."

The town is no longer on the map, but the six-mile stretch of country road that bears its name has become legendary. It seems that throughout its history, Sinnet Road has been taking people to destinations truly "unknown."

Here are three of the better-known Sinnet Road stories.

It was February 1938, and a young man named Gerry walked along Sinnet Road one evening, on his way to play penny-ante poker with some friends. He was bundled against the cold; his boots crunching in the snow. It was a lonely sound, breaking the frosty silence.

Sinnet Road ran past a cemetery, and as Gerry came closer to it, he could see a man in the distance, approaching. "That must be Keller," he thought, expecting it to be a local fellow who wanted to join in the game. He called out a greeting.

The man showed no sign of hearing Gerry, but continued to walk towards him. Gerry must have thought his words were lost on the wind, and tried speaking to his friend again.

Again, there was no reply.

When Gerry was directly in front of the cemetery, and the man he thought to be his friend was no more than twenty yards away, he called out to him one last time. "Hey, Keller!" he shouted; but the words were barely past his lips before he knew he had made a mistake.

Not only was this not Mr. Keller, it was not any ordinary person. As Gerry's words hung in the cold night air, the man who had been walking toward him transformed, unbelievably, into a huge fireball which flew up high, over the cemetery gate and telephone wires, then descended, still flaming, and disappeared among the tombstones.

Gerry still attended that night's poker game but, chances are, he didn't play. His friends reported that he walked in the door looking as white as the snow outside. He was shaking violently, and couldn't speak for quite some time.

Once Gerry did talk, however, this was the tale he told. Decades later, his story lives on as one of the legends of Sinnet Road.

Imagine yourself driving northbound on Sinnet Road, late at night. You see car lights approaching, and watch them disappear as the south-bound driver enters the gully, just beyond the bridge. You watch the car's headlights reflecting off cloud-cover in the sky, as it climbs the hill, on its way towards you. You pull over as far as possible, hoping the shoulder's not too soft, and dim your lights, knowing that you're about to meet the other vehicle. But as you crest the hill, and the small valley comes into full view before you, you're shocked to discover that you're alone on this dark stretch of narrow country road.

This is the ghost car of Sinnet Road.

Time after time, people reported having this strange encounter. These accounts may have been disregarded, but tracks in the mud or snow frequently offered proof, at least, of the storyteller's conviction. Because Sinnet Road was so narrow and poorly maintained, pulling over meant taking the risk of getting stuck. You only did it if you were sure, *very* sure, of meeting another vehicle.

The next time you see approaching headlights wink out behind a hill, or a stand of trees, imagine that the ghost car of Sinnet Road is coming your way.

It was around ten o'clock one winter evening, in the late 1970s, and Jim and Doris Belger's (pseudonyms) son Peter had just arrived home from high school volleyball practice. Though he appeared to be fine, physically, he had come in the house trembling and pale and was now pacing the floor frantically, mumbling to himself and peering cautiously out the windows.

"He was terrified," Doris later said. "and it took awhile for him to tell us why."

When Peter was calm enough to speak, he told his parents that he had been driving up Sinnet Road, towards the farm, when he saw a "thing" come up out of the ditch. He slowed the car and tried to get a better view. When Peter was close enough to see the creature, it dashed across the road in front of him, illuminated briefly by the car's head-lights.

"And what was it?" Doris and Jim asked, breathlessly.

Peter answered: "A big hairy man."

There was a beat of silence, following Peter's dramatic disclosure, then his parents burst into laughter.

"Oh, for heaven's sake, Peter," gasped his mother, "you should have stopped! Maybe somebody ran out of gas and needed your help!"

Making light of the situation should have made Peter realize that his teenage imagination had simply overtaken his common sense. But instead, he became more upset, screaming "You won't laugh when you're murdered in your own bed tonight!" Seeing his obvious fear, and knowing that their son was usually a level-headed boy, the Belgers began to take his story seriously. They complied when he insisted upon calling the neighbours, warning them to lock their doors, and they locked and barred their own. Still, that night, Peter insisted upon taking a hunting knife into the bedroom he shared with his brother.

Cool heads often prevail in the light of day, and by the next morning, Jim and Doris Belger were quite convinced that Peter had suffered nothing more than an encounter with a black bear and a fitful night's sleep. Indeed, he seemed calmer, although he refused to accept his parents' rational explanations.

"I know what I saw," he insisted. "It was like a monster. A big, hairy man with a hunched back."

And so, the matter was dropped. At least for a couple of days, until a particular news item on the radio caught the family's interest.

Apparently, there had been a Sasquatch sighted, just over one hundred miles east of the Belger farm, near Theodore. Of course, the reporter had assembled the facts and *deduced* it was a Sasquatch.

The witness, it seems, could only describe it as a "big hairy man."

The Silent Organ

Some time ago, the Assiniboia and District Historical Society came into possession of an antique pump organ. It had been poorly stored over the years, and came laden with dust, leaves and bird droppings. It also came with a fascinating story.

Today, the organ has been beautifully cleaned and restored, and is on display in the Society's museum. As for the story, Lila Martinson was kind enough to share it.

The Trivetts were among many families of British descent that settled first in Ontario, then migrated west. In 1908, with their five children in tow, Mr. and Mrs. Trivett came to a new life on a new homestead, near the now-extinct town of Readlyn, Saskatchewan.

Mary Trivett must have been the embodiment of the unflappable constitution her forefathers made famous. Surely, as the mother of five and a busy farm wife, her days were filled with hard work and worries. Still, she was always able to help a neighbour or take on a new challenge, and her ability to "be British" in the face of adversity made her a valued member of the community.

All her life, Mary had been a devoted member of the Salvation Army. In Readlyn there was no branch of her beloved organization, but such a trivial detail could never have kept the determined Mrs. Trivett from carrying out their charitable doctrine. Her home was always open to the poor and outcast, her kindnesses were known to friends and strangers alike, and throughout World War I, all of Readlyn benefitted from her strenuous wartime efforts.

Much of Mary's good work was accomplished through her affiliation with the United Church. She enjoyed the church and its people immensely, but confessed once to the organist, Walter Eaglestone, that she dearly missed the energizing drums and tambourines associated with the Salvation Army.

"When I go," she confided to him, "I don't want the organ played at my funeral." Apparently, Mary felt that the traditional sombre music would not be appropriately indicative of her upbeat life.

Walter Eaglestone may have dismissed the comment as casual conversation, or he may have simply forgotten it with time. Whatever the reason, when Mary Trivett passed away in the spring of 1928, her request was overlooked. Walter, still being the United Church's most accomplished organist, prepared a number of moving hymns for Mary's funeral.

The day of the service came, and mourners began filing into the church. At this cue, Walter selected his first hymn and began to play.

Strangely, the organ didn't make a sound.

Confused, Walter tried playing the notes again. The only thing to be heard was the shuffling of Mary's many friends, as they took places in the pews.

Walter gave the organ a discreet examination and found nothing apparently wrong with it. Indeed, it had played beautifully just hours before, as Walter diligently practised the hymns. But now, no matter how he pumped the pedals or what keys he played, the instrument remained mysteriously mute. Finally, the frustrated man gave up, and Mary Trivett's funeral service continued without musical accompaniment.

Following the interment, Walter returned to the church, hoping to solve the puzzle. With the first note he struck, however, music filled the room. Amazingly, the organ played just as it had up to the moment when Mary's funeral began.

And suddenly, it made sense.

Everything became clear to Walter, as he remembered the woman's words of long ago. Mary had not wanted the organ played at her funeral and so, it had not played. Somehow, this determined lady had seen to it that her one last wish was fulfilled.

Today, as this beautiful instrument sits on display in Assiniboia, we are reminded of one woman's staunch spirit. The silent organ honoured Mary Trivett as no hymn ever could.

Hauntings are common. Hauntings are very, very common. Much more than I ever would have imagined.

Dr. Buddy Wynn, Parapsychologist

University of Regina

September 26, 1994

The St. Louis Ghost Train

Spend fifteen minutes in the Village of St. Louis, Saskatchewan, and you'll know what its residents hold dear. In the local coffee shop, there are three portraits hanging side by side: Louis Riel, Gabriel Dumont and Guy LaFleur. There's a huge billboard on the main street, greeting visitors with its colourful depiction of a local boy who made good in the NHL. And then there's the ghost train ...

The St. Louis ghost train; it's one of Saskatchewan's famous phantoms, having received a great deal of press and even national television coverage. The residents of the tiny village seem quietly proud of their supernatural attraction; nearly anyone on the street can offer up the details. The story is unusual, in that the legend has been passed down for generations, but the phenomenon is still active today.

THE BRIDGE IN THE DISTANCE ONCE TOOK TRAINS DIRECTLY INTO ST. LOUIS. NOW, IT ONLY CARRIES CARS ... AND STORIES.

A few miles north of St. Louis is a flat stretch of land that was once a railway bed. The tracks were pulled up long ago, but the route is still followed by what many believe to be a spectral train.

The apparition is unfailingly described as a huge beam of white light; reminiscent of the headlights on old-fashioned trains. It follows the land as the tracks once did, and has been seen approaching St. Louis by hundreds of witnesses over the years, including the village's mayor. Many people offer their own personal accounts of the light, as well as stories handed down to them by their parents and grandparents. Naturally, with these stories come popular theories regarding the origin of the beacon.

Most of the rumours circulated involve the horrible demise of a conductor or engineer. Legend has it that the unfortunate man was doing a routine check of the tracks, when he was struck down by a train and decapitated. Locals say the light is a sign that he is still looking for his head. In a 1990 issue of the *Prince Albert Daily Herald*, St. Louis resident Pat Boyer summed up the ironic futility of such a search, saying "he'll never find it because his head and eyes are gone."

Another theory also involves an accident and one of the railway workers. This account is of a man who would wave a lantern, signalling the trains when they needed to switch tracks. He was accidentally run over by one of the locomotives, and people speculate that the light is his phantom lantern, still trying to warn the engineers of impending disaster.

While these stories are highly dramatic, they don't quite fit the phenomenon; after all, the light of an approaching train is quite distinguishable from that of a hand-held lantern. Some St. Louis residents think the best explanation for the train may be that it's a "psychic imprint" of sorts.

"That train came around that bend so many times, it probably wore a groove into something," said one woman. But whatever the explanation behind St. Louis's ghost train, there's little doubt that it creates some strange occurrences.

Chris McLeod is a young man who grew up in Prince Albert, just a short drive north of St. Louis. When he was in high school, Chris and his friends discovered that they could make an inexpensive evening's entertainment of driving out to view the ghost train. They became frequent visitors, and daring ones, as well.

"One of the unwritten rules of the St. Louis light is that you never park your car on the tracks. Being the immortal adolescent that I was, I sometimes did just that," Chris wrote to me. This act of defiance generally produced small problems; the windshield wipers would spontaneously turn on, the headlights on the car would flicker, and sometimes it would be difficult to restart the engine.

One winter night in 1987, Chris and a friend drove out to see the light. They parked their car where the tracks once were and, perhaps anticipating that it might be troublesome restarting it, left the engine running.

"We didn't have to wait long," said Chris of the apparition. "It showed up after about two minutes." The teens only watched the approaching light for roughly thirty seconds, however, before something else seized their attention.

Chris and his friend saw what they thought to be steam billowing out from under the hood. Thinking the radiator had boiled over, they shut off the ignition and rushed outside to take a look at the engine. One deep breath told them that it wasn't steam they were dealing with, it was smoke. The cause appeared to be a fire in the alternator.

"We had no way of extinguishing an electrical fire, so we decided to blow it out on the highway," Chris recalls. They made the return trip at speeds of over 120 kilometres per hour, and did not stop until they safely reached Prince Albert.

Interestingly, the electrical system gave them no problems on the way home, and the mechanic who fixed the car admitted he could not figure out what happened. The alternator was replaced, despite the fact that nothing defective about it was discovered.

To this day, Chris McLeod remains fascinated by the St. Louis light. "I have heard scientific explanations for the ghost light, and someday I would like to try to prove these theories." In this, he is not alone.

There have been frequent attempts, by photographers, to capture the apparition on film. The results have been interesting, if not conclusive. In one particular case a number of pictures were taken, but the entire film turned out blank white, with the exception of two small red dots that were described as looking like "eyes."

Don MacPhedran, a volunteer with the Prince Albert Historical Museum, claims to have used his camera equipment to debunk the theory of the phantom light. In the February 29, 1992 edition of the *Prince Albert Daily Herald*, MacPhedran explained his ideas in a letter to the editor:

> The lights are vehicle lights that appear and
> then disappear owing to the changes in the
> elevation of the highway. They are plainly visible
> with a high-power telephoto lens or a good field
> glass.

St. Louis residents scoff at MacPhedran's theory, however, claiming to have long ago tested it for themselves by flashing car lights at various points on the highway and recording the appearance of these lights by the track. The conclusion was that the tiny, distant headlights bore no resemblance to the huge, white beacon that so many have witnessed.

The possibility of vehicle lights was also addressed by Pat Boyer, in the *Prince Albert Daily Herald.*

"My great-grandmother, she remembers when she was a teenager, people talking about the light," he said. "When she was a teenager, there weren't any cars."

And so a multi-generational mystery continues, in the unassuming village of St. Louis, Saskatchewan.

The Ghost in Government House

Government House in Regina, built in 1881, has the distinction of being one of the few remaining territorial government buildings.

In its long lifetime, it has served as residence for the lieutenant-governors of the Northwest Territories and, after 1905, of Saskatchewan. Following the Second World War, financial woes contributed to the building's transformation to a veterans' hospital, under the new name of "Saskatchewan House." Twenty years later, it provided a shared home for Community College, Little Theatre and the Arts Board.

Today, Government House has reverted to fulfilling its original purpose. Although it is no longer used as a residence, the grand building once again houses the offices of the lieutenant-governor. And if you ask the right people, you'll find that it provides one other important service.

It is home to a ghost.

Every October in Regina, troops of schoolchildren make their way to Government House for an hour of speculation and fun. It's "Hallowe'en with Howie," an inspired program that captures the kids' imaginations while sneaking in a little history lesson on the sly.

"Howie," as he is known, is the legendary ghost of Government House. Children are entertained by video-taped reports of his antics, then taken on a tour of the House, stopping at points where spooky incidents have taken place. Afterward, there are ghostly word games to play, and an opportunity to make a "Howie Lolly" out of a lollipop and a tissue.

It may sound like a tame concoction of seasonal entertainment for the children, but there are many who swear that Howie is real. He has a reputation for mischief, but has never truly frightened anyone; seeming to be the spectral equivalent of a big, friendly, toothless dog – completely lovable, and a threat to no one.

GOVERNMENT HOUSE IN REGINA: AN HISTORIC SITE AND MUSEUM,
OFFICE TO SASKATCHEWAN'S LIEUTENANT-GOVERNOR, AND HOME
TO A POPULAR GHOST.

Staff members who have worked nights in Government House claim that Howie likes to make his presence known in a number of ways. Toilets will flush, quite autonomously, when the hour is late. If you use the rear stairway, it is said that there is a strong sense of someone being there with you. Doors have been seen unlatching and swinging open, and it has become routine to have something disappear from its usual place, only to reappear, days later.

Keeping track of Howie's pranks is only part of the fun, however. In a building that boasts the dramatic history of Government House, it is equally intriguing to speculate about the phantom's identity.

In a Hallowe'en with Howie Teacher Guide, Bob Burke, a former historian for Government House Heritage Property, shared some of his theories. Burke felt that Howie might have been a previous governor who had taken out a "spiritual lease" on his former residence. Perhaps he was one of the many soldiers who convalesced there, after the war. And considering the possibility that Howie could be a female, he wondered if they weren't dealing with the spirit of a former chamber-maid. That would explain the occasional unexplained spots of cleaning and polishing that have been found around the House.

The most widely accepted explanation, however, concerns a Chinese cook named Cheun, who worked for Lieutenant-Governor Archibald McNab in the 1940s. Cheun contracted pneumonia, while in residence, and died in a back bedroom of the House. It wasn't long after that the staff began hearing the whispery sounds of Cheun's slippers, roaming about the servant's quarters at night.

No matter who Howie was in his earthly existence, in his spiritual form he has become a beloved fixture at Government House. Bob Burke, in the Hallowe'en with Howie Teacher Guide, expressed the sentiment best:

> We have become accustomed to his mischievous
> ways and rather enjoy them. Howie has entered
> our lives and made a permanent place in our
> hearts. If, one day, Howie were to depart for
> other realms, Government House would never quite
> be the same – something wonderful would have
> passed from our lives.

And so, Saskatchewan's best-loved ghost continues to live the high life, in the stately mansion that is Government House.

Footsteps at Fairlight

On the eastern edge of what Tourism Saskatchewan calls "Horizon Country" is the small community of Fairlight. One of Fairlight's nearby farms was homesteaded early in the century by Harold Potvin (a pseudonym), a man who dearly loved his land until the day he died.

Unfortunately, that day came early for Harold. He was a young fifty-six-year-old when he passed away, bequeathing his cherished farm to family. Through the years, Harold's children and grandchildren continued to work the land, but each branch of the family had its own home, so the house that their patriarch had built, lived and died in was left sitting empty.

At least, that's what they thought.

It was harvest time, and as he did every fall, Kevin Potvin found himself working almost unbearably long days. He was in the fields at the crack of dawn, and seldom home until an hour or so after the sun had set. He loved farming, but each September he wondered if he had bitten off more than he could chew. After all, it wasn't just his own section; he tended to his late Grandpa Harold's land, too.

One night, Kevin worked later than usual on his grandfather's farm. An uncle and cousin who were lending a hand had left an hour earlier, and Kevin found himself alone and exhausted as he shut down the combine. The twenty-minute drive back to his own tiny trailer seemed insuperable, not to mention impractical, considering he would only enjoy a few hours sleep before having to return at first light. He thought he had found a practical solution when he decided to stay right where he was, and sleep in Grandpa Harold's deserted house.

Although the two-storey farm house hadn't been used in years, it was a sound structure that hadn't fallen into disrepair. Doors and windows remained intact; floors and walls met solidly. Certainly, there was a lack of regular housekeeping, but Kevin was much too tired to mind the dust. He gratefully lugged his sleeping bag from the cab of his pickup truck to the bedroom at the top of the wide, wooden staircase. There, on the antique wrought iron bed, he succumbed to his fatigue.

Seemingly moments later, Kevin was wrenched from unconsciousness.

Brief panic welled in him when he couldn't immediately identify his surroundings. As the feeling gave way to recognition, he dazedly wondered what could have awakened him with such a start.

"Just overtired," he mumbled to himself, settling back down. As he closed his eyes he seemed to remember a vague dream, the sound of forceful pounding on the floor.

But he wasn't dreaming now.

It was so loud, there was no mistaking the sound of those heavy footfalls on the stairs. Wide-eyed and now quite awake, Kevin sat up and held his breath, waiting to meet the intruder. He listened intensely as the footsteps paused at the top of the stairs and then proceeded the short distance down the hall to his room. He steeled himself for a confrontation, waited tensely for the door to burst open, but, strangely, nothing happened.

It was several minutes before he found the courage to open the door himself. When he did, he faced nothing more frightening than a dark and empty hallway. Cursing himself for his own foolishness, Kevin went back to bed, determined to get the sleep he so desperately needed.

His eyes had barely shut, however, when the mysterious footsteps started again, at the bottom of the stairs.

"So there *is* someone there!" he thought. "This time I'll catch him in the act!" Kevin slipped silently out of bed and tip-toed across the bedroom. As the stomping feet reached the top of the staircase, he threw open the bedroom door.

There was nothing. And after all, how could there be? ... because the moonlight pouring in through the windows showed only one set of footprints in the thick dust on the stairs, and they belonged to Kevin.

Shaken, he returned to his bed. Almost immediately, the haunting sound began again.

By two o'clock in the morning, Kevin had taken to counting the number of stairs his unseen visitor climbed on each trip, as well as the number of heavy steps taken from the top of the staircase to the doorway of his bedroom. By 4:00 AM, he decided to try sleeping in his truck. Two hours later, Kevin's uncle arrived and the work day began.

"You look like hell," the uncle stated, when he saw the dark circles under Kevin's bloodshot eyes. "What were you doing after you got home, last night?"

"I didn't go home," said Kevin. "I saved some driving time and stayed here, in the house." He left his explanation at that, not wanting to be ridiculed about what he had just experienced.

Kevin's uncle shook his head solemnly. "You're braver than I am," he said. Warily, Kevin asked him what he meant.

"I tried staying here once, a couple years ago," the uncle explained. "Never got a wink of sleep. I kept hearing this stomping on the stairs. Sounded like the heavy old work boots that Dad used to wear."

Harold Potvin lived and died as a hard-working farmer, and it would seem that even now, he hates to see anyone rest when the fields need tending.

Reason and science have traditionally had an uneasy relationship with mysteries. Mysteries are the lure for scientists, but mysteries that refuse to be solved are often tossed into the realm of fancy and impossibility.

Dave Geary

Broadway Magazine

September-October 1994

Holy Ghosts

Until the early nineteenth century, paranormal phenomenon and organized religion were inextricably bound together as mutually reinforcing matters of faith. The last two hundred years has seen an official separation of the two, although unofficially, Western culture seems to be adopting a broader, more inclusive form of spirituality.

Perhaps as a result of this new openness, or as validation of more superstitious, outdated beliefs, churches are common backdrops for supernatural occurrences. The following three stories come from the Prince Albert area alone, and may be indicative of more widespread phenomenon.

Lisa Boisvert (a pseudonym) was twelve years old, and as excited as any twelve-year-old girl can be when there's a sleep-over planned for the weekend. She had an overnight bag packed, and when the school bell rang at the end of a seemingly endless Friday, Lisa walked home with her best friend, Molly.

Overnight stays at Molly's place were always a little more interesting because of the unusual home her family owned. It had, at one time, been a church with an attached rectory. Services had not been held there for years, though, and the rectory now served as a private residence with an unusual "addition."

The girls loved to spend time in the church. It provided them with a private place to gossip and tell secrets, and offered perfect acoustics when they felt like singing their favourite songs. Lisa, who had taken years of piano lessons, loved the fact that the grand pipe organ still played beautifully, and remained in its place of honour off to the side of the pulpit.

Just past midnight, after hours of junk food, conversation and games, the girls decided to turn in. Lisa had difficulty sleeping, and as she tossed and turned in the unfamiliar bed, her thoughts eventually turned to the lovely organ in the church. She regretted not having found an opportunity to play earlier that evening. "Well, why not now?" she mused. Everyone else in the house was asleep, but Lisa knew from experience that the walls were well sound-proofed and she would not be disturbing a soul.

SASKATCHEWAN IS HOME TO A NUMBER OF BEAUTIFULLY RESTORED
CHURCHES, INCLUDING THIS ONE AT BATOCHE NATIONAL HISTORIC
PARK. PERHAPS ONE DAY, WE'LL KNOW HOW MANY OF THESE
RELIGIOUS SITES ARE HOUSING EARTH-BOUND SPIRITS AND
PARANORMAL PHENOMENON.

Silently, she crept into the darkened church, careful to shut the connecting door behind her. It felt good to slide onto the cool, highly polished surface of the wooden bench and rest her fingers on the keys. In her mind she scanned a list of popular songs that she knew by heart, but none of them seemed to suit the moment. Finally, she selected a gentle hymn taught to her as a little girl, and, eyes half-closed, began to play.

The music swelled to fill the room, and Lisa swayed slightly on the bench, feeling the keys instead of looking at them. She was playing well, perhaps even beyond her years of instruction, and she marvelled at how easily the music was coming to her. The moment Lisa opened her eyes, however, she discovered something far more remarkable.

Later, she would describe them as spirits or entities, for that's what she felt they were. They appeared to her as soft points of white light, materializing at the church's front door and floating, in line, down the aisle.

Lisa continued to play, afraid of breaking the spell, and the glowing apparitions continued to enter the church. When there were approximately twenty in all, they broke formation to take places in the pews, and stayed obediently still. Incredibly, they seemed to be listening.

Showing impressive calm for a twelve-year-old girl, Lisa finished playing the hymn. Then, unable to think of another suitably inspirational selection, she sat quietly with her hands in her lap and watched as, one by one, the beautiful lights winked out.

There was a pervading sense of peace when they were gone, and Lisa retreated to the house to sleep dreamlessly for the rest of the night. The event felt special and significant, and it was days before she shared the story of her appreciative spiritual audience with anyone.

Today, Lisa is a teenager who remembers the incident vividly, but has experienced nothing like it since.

On the narrow stretch of highway between Prince Albert and St. Louis, there is a parcel of land that is rumoured to hold a terrible secret. Locally, it is known as the Church of the Singing Nuns, and although the musical reference is curious, the strict mores of the Catholic Church play an obvious part.

According to legend, a young nun from a local convent became pregnant. Unable to accept this embarrassing development, the other sisters rationalized that the baby must certainly be the work of Satan. When it was born, they took the innocent child and disposed of it by throwing it down a well.

That well sits on the aforementioned property along the highway. Believers in the legend contend that if you stop by the spot, there will be a sign of your pilgrimage.

You see, visitors to the Church of the Singing Nuns come away with tiny little hand-prints on their vehicles.

I met a young woman in downtown Prince Albert who was enjoying her coffee break out of doors on an unseasonably hot September afternoon. We began talking about haunted churches, and she mentioned St. Catherine's Anglican Church, "about five miles west of the Pen."

She said it had once been a favourite location for teenagers' parties, and that she had been there several times during her own high school years.

"It was always on a dare," she told me. "We were absolutely terrified of the place, so it was exciting to hang out in the churchyard and drink a beer or two."

The fear was fed chiefly by rumours. "They" said that a priest committed suicide there, and was sometimes seen pacing the floor. "They" maintained that black masses had been held in the building, although no one knew who officiated or when it might have happened. "They" had all kinds of deliciously dark stories about the church, passed from person to person, over the years.

Interestingly, I had already heard of the church by way of the John M. Cuelenaere Library, in Prince Albert. Carole Naylor, Head of the Audio-Visual and Periodical Department, wrote a letter that included this bit of folklore: "The story was, that, if you rang the church bell twelve times just before midnight on Halloween, the bell would give thirteen chimes."

This particular tale earned St. Catherine's Anglican Church the catchy nickname "Hell's Bells."

Unfortunately, the church was burned to the ground by an arsonist a few years ago. The dramatic stories still float around, but the source of the legends is gone.

The Restless Spirit of Bickleigh

UNTIL A YOUNG MAN'S REMAINS WERE UNEARTHED, THESE FIELDS
NEAR BICKLEIGH WERE HAUNTED.

*The tiny village of Bickleigh was once home to a ghost. Now, it is barely
a ghost town, having disappeared entirely from the Saskatchewan map.*

*The following story was first documented by Mary O. McLean in a
1991 local history book. Hazel J. McCloskey of the Prairie West Historical
Society in Eston kindly sent it my way.*

The people who lived in Bickleigh may have been considered by
their neighbours to be a superstitious lot. For a place its tiny
size, Bickleigh seemed to have a disproportionately large number of ghost stories. There were tales of apparitions and unexplained
sounds and, frequently, residents swore they could sense an eerie presence when they were supposedly alone.

After nearly sixty years of being haunted, a grisly discovery and some interesting historical facts led these people to believe that every unexplainable story and each spooky feeling had been the work of one restless spirit; a spirit that had, over time, become known as "The Bickleigh Ghost."

The first reported sighting of The Bickleigh Ghost came in 1932. Two sisters, Ivy and Annie Bristow, were enjoying a moonlit sleigh ride home, following an evening visit with some neighbours. As they approached the railway crossing, the horses suddenly snorted loudly, and refused to move any further. The Bristow sisters stood up to find out what was frightening the team and were astonished to see a spectral horse and rider, galloping along the track at full speed. The apparition was misty in the moonlight, and absolutely silent, even as it passed directly in front of them. Once the ghost had sped out of sight, the horses hitched to the sleigh bolted, and, without prompting, ran the rest of the way to the Bristow farm. Ivy and Annie spent the remainder of the trip casting wide-eyed glances over their shoulders, making sure that whatever they saw wasn't following them home.

The following summer, an equally unsettling experience was shared by a school teacher, Joe Pitzel, and the local Pool agent, Joe Ellis. The two young men shared a room in a Bickleigh boarding house. They each had a single bed, and between the beds stood a small table, which served as a shared nightstand. The table was covered with a heavily starched cloth, and was used to hold a variety of the men's personal items. At the very back of the table stood a coal oil lamp.

One night, the men had just extinguished the lamp and settled into their beds when they both heard articles fall off the table. At first, it was a few coins hitting the floor boards and rolling to their resting places. Then, it was the heavier clatter of a pocket knife, and the hollow rattle of a pen. Both Pitzel and Ellis jumped from their beds, scrambled for the box of matches and, with shaking hands, lit one. The flickering circle of pale yellow light illuminated a strange scene. The lamp, which always sat at the back of the table, was teetering on the front edge, ready to fall. The starched cloth was bunched and crumpled, as if a hand had grasped it and pulled it forward, letting all the items on the table drop as it moved.

The two men lit the lamp and examined the small room for any other signs of disturbance, but they found none. The bedroom door had remained firmly shut throughout the incident, as was the window. No explanation was ever found.

Some time later, Joe Pitzel had another encounter with The Bickleigh Ghost. He and the United Grain Growers agent, Mac McLean, were sharing an early supper. Mac's living quarters were attached to the engine room, which was four steps below the office. The men had barely begun to eat when they distinctly heard the office door open. Someone then walked across the creaky floor of the office, came down the four steps, and stopped directly outside the door to Mac's apartment.

"Come on in!" yelled Mac, assuming it was a friend. There was no answer, so he called out again. The reply was silence.

"Someone's trying to scare us," said Joe, rising from his chair. "Let's find out who it is."

They opened the door and found no one. The two men separated, and conducted a quick but thorough search of the office, the engine room and the area surrounding the elevator. When they were done, their only explanation was that they had been visited by the ghost.

A farmer named George Redhead never heard of The Bickleigh Ghost, yet had an experience that was strangely reminiscent of that of the Bristow sisters. George purchased a half-section of land through which the railroad ran. While he was breaking the soil, he would work until the last daylight had bled away, then sleep for a few hours in his truck canopy, which he had placed on the ground. One night, he had barely made himself comfortable when he was alarmed by the rapidly approaching sound of thundering hooves. The ground shook with the relentless pounding and George worried that the rider wouldn't notice his little makeshift shelter. Fearing that he was about to be trampled, he scrambled out of his bedding and from under the truck canopy. There, in the cool night air, his panic turned to confusion; for although he clearly heard the horse gallop by him, there was nothing to be seen. It was a perfectly clear night, lit by the full moon, yet as the sound of hooves receded in the distance, George could see neither horse nor rider.

A few miles beyond George Redhead's land, the railway tracks ran past an old, abandoned house. Two men who ventured inside one day, searching for antiques, claimed to have had their own encounter with The Bickleigh Ghost. They were poking around in the cellar when they heard the front door open and someone walk across the main floor. They quickly ran upstairs to see who it was, but found the house as empty as when they came in. Thinking that whoever it had been may be in the yard, they took a look outside. There were no other buildings on the land, and no trees. The two antique-hunters could see for miles in every direction, and easily determined that they were alone, at least in terms of human company. Spooked by the experience, they gave up their search and hastily returned to town.

In 1980, the section of railroad that ran past Bickleigh was abandoned. In 1981, the rails and ties were taken up; some destined for reuse in the railroad yards, the rest sold to a razor blade company. It was the end of an era.

Just one year later, in 1982, a farmer's gruesome find brought the deceased tracks a final measure of attention. Bruce McDonald was cultivating a field just a half-mile south of the railway bed when he noticed a large white rock. As he moved to toss it out of his way, he was shocked to discover that it was actually a human skull, gleaming in the sunlight. Further investigation turned up a leg bone, arm bone and a rib, all of which were handed over to the RCMP.

The Department of Anthropology at the University of Saskatchewan determined what was possible from this very incomplete skeleton. The facial bone structure was that of a Caucasian male. The fusion of the leg bone, which occurs at maturity, suggested that the man was approximately twenty-five years old at the time of death. Experts also felt that the remains had lain in the field for about sixty years. It was this final number that reminded Bickleigh residents of a long-forgotten story.

It was 1924 when the railroad was extended from Milden to McMorran. By the time construction reached Bickleigh, winter had set in. Normally difficult working conditions became almost unbearable; horses were literally worked to death and buried in the track bed, and stress heaped upon the men caused tempers to flare on a regular basis.

One night, a particularly bitter fight broke out between two workers. Mysteriously, one of them had disappeared by the following morning and was never heard from again. There were suspicions and talk of foul play. Someone suggested digging in the track bed for a body. However, because of the harsh conditions, men had been known to simply walk off the job. People must have chosen to believe this less disturbing scenario, as the incident was eventually forgotten.

The young man who had vanished was twenty-five years old; the approximate age of death experts determined after studying the skeletal remains. He disappeared in 1924; the remains were found in 1982, and were believed to have been there for about sixty years. Could there be a connection?

Locals seem to believe that the skull and few bones belonged to the railway worker, and that he was murdered in 1924. Further, they believe him to be The Bickleigh Ghost, trying desperately for sixty years to tell people he was not at rest.

Hopefully he is now, having been granted a decent, albeit anonymous, burial.

Old Faithful: The Tabor Light

THE TABOR CEMETERY: HOME TO ONE OF SASKATCHEWAN'S MOST
FAMOUS PHANTOM LIGHTS.

One of Saskatchewan's most famous, and certainly most documented, supernatural tales is this account of a strange light that has haunted a cemetery near Esterhazy since nearly the turn of the century.

1905

The wind is still icy today, and though the rain has stopped, the sky remains a compassionless gun-metal grey. Deep ruts line the mucky country road, and, for the lone horse pulling a rickety wagon, the going is slow.

The young man in the driver's seat is miserably cold in his thin, black, cloth coat. Even without the tell-tale white collar at his throat, one would imagine him to be a fellow who works with his brain, not his brawn. His hands are pale, soft and beginning to chafe from tugging at the reins for the last eighteen miles.

He reaches his destination; a raw-looking graveyard surrounded by brush and farmers' fields. There is no church overlooking it, no religious insignia on the rough boards that serve as a gate. The priest knows that there are some graves which no one has bothered to even mark. It is for one of these, he has come.

He casts a worried glance up and down the lonely road, to ensure he has no company. He climbs down off the wagon, and walks to the side of the road, but no further. Following another hasty look around, the man clasps his hands and begins furtively to pray.

1923

The bridge game was lively, and the gaiety of the evening caused her to leave a little later than she had planned. Still, it's no concern. This night is lovely for a ride, with its warm air on her cheek and the lazy clip-clop of the horse's hooves on the hard-packed dirt road.

There's no moon to be seen; even the cemetery ahead is drowned in dark shadows. The individual shapes of the grave markers are lost. Suddenly, the night air is slightly more chilled, and she looks around uncomfortably.

It's there.

A reddish globe of light, trailing behind her, on the road.

Fearfully, she tugs at the reins, forcing her horse into a brisk canter. The mysterious light increases its speed, maintaining position, behind her. She digs her heels into the horse's side and issues a sharp command. It breaks into a run. But every step taken is matched by the phantom light.

It is several terrifying, eternal minutes before she gallops into her own yard, leaps off the horse and dives behind the safety of her heavy kitchen door. Finally, the glowing orb disappears in the night.

1935

Heavy clouds are swallowing tonight's moon and stars, and the young farm boy is nervous as he walks home from a neighbour's house, along a lonely, black stretch of road. He has a gun with him, but he wishes more for company; some conversation to distract him as he walks past the cemetery.

Suddenly, it's there, a ghostly globe of pale fire on the snowy road ahead of him. Worse, it's speeding towards him, bearing down on him, and the twelve-gauge shotgun feels like a thousand pounds as he lifts it to his shoulder and squeezes the trigger.

The sound of the blast echoes in the night. Terrified and exhilarated, the trembling boy walks down the road to the spot where the light died.

He finds nothing but untrampled snow.

1938

It's festive here, tonight. Another car pulls up, honking to announce its arrival, and the jug of moonshine gets passed around again. Some of the women have put together lunch pails full of sandwiches and pickled preserves, but most are too excited to eat.

There are over eighty people at the cemetery tonight. Someone yells at the driver of the newly arrived vehicle to turn off his headlights. With all the flashlights and brilliantly popping bulbs from the reporters' cameras, it will be a miracle if they see anything. Yet, they hope. And every time someone lights a cigarette in the distance, they jump.

The Tabor Cemetery, seventeen miles northeast of Esterhazy, qualifies as one of Saskatchewan's most haunted places. Over decades, it has been visited frequently by an unexplainable phantom light. The light appeared so regularly, in fact, that nearby residents chose to dub it "Old Faithful."

The Tabor Light was sometimes described as a ball of fire, slightly reddish or pinkish in color, and occasionally flickering. Witnesses always said the glow appeared to be directed inward; the light never illuminated the surrounding area. It's size was estimated to be roughly that of a ten-quart pail, it was capable of appearing and disappearing magically, and it would either dance among the trees skirting the cemetery, or speed along the road that ran past it. Sometimes it moved towards people; sometimes away, keeping a consistent distance in front of its pursuer. On one occasion, in what may qualify as the closest sighting ever reported, a couple claimed the light actually passed through the back seat of their car.

Although Old Faithful stayed true to its name and made regular appearances at the Tabor Cemetery, it took more than thirty years to become an overnight sensation. In the late fall of 1938, it became a celebrity of at least provincial proportions, drawing people from all over southern Saskatchewan. Newspapers took a great interest, and the light frequently enjoyed front page status.

The crowds grew as the publicity did. By Thursday, December 1,

1938, attendance records were beginning to be set as 100 thrill-seekers showed up to spend a cold night at this newly famous graveyard. By Sunday, reporters were thinking to check licence plates and found several vehicles from Manitoba and one from Ontario, a testament to the far-reaching appeal of this unsolvable riddle.

Local teenagers usually made up a part of the crowd. They had discovered quite a practical use for the Tabor Light; it provided the perfect location and excuse for a curfew-breaking date. In the December 2, 1938 edition of the *Regina Leader-Post*, it was written that "Young boys and girls, questioned by their parents as to their late hours merely say they were hunting the spook and the matter is cleared up without another word. The result is Tabor has become, not only the most popular meeting place for miles around, but also a centre for prolific billing and cooing."

Chances are, those young people taking advantage of the fervor surrounding Tabor Cemetery knew little of its interesting history. It was founded in 1903 by a small group of Bohemian settlers who had become bitterly and openly anti-religious. The desolate site, miles from any church, was chosen so that no clergymen could oversee their funerals. In its first years of existence, it was known to some as "the pagan cemetery," because people were buried there without the ministrations of a priest.

Such behaviour was highly suspect to the people of the area who clung to simple religious values. When the phantom light was first seen, the general opinion was that it was the embodied souls of those buried in Tabor, unable to rest in peace. Suspicions grew about the atheistic faction of the Bohemian community, and wild stories spread about sudden disappearances, and secret, illegal, midnight burials. Later, as the anti-religious fervor of the early 1900s was forgotten, other equally superstitious theories took hold.

One story hinted strongly at a murder by poison that was thought to have taken place around 1908. It was greeted sceptically by authorities, who offered the supposed victim's certificate of death as proof. The people stood by their story, however, amending it to include the imaginative explanation that no ordinary poison had been used, but a potion that would be invisible in any post-mortem examination of the body. It was further suggested that along with this deadly concoction were strange and special powers, handed down for generations within a certain family in the area.

By 1938, as crowds gathered to catch a glimpse of the now-famous light, farmers in the area shared one common theory regarding its reason for being. They saw it as an omen; a harbinger of doom. One man, who claimed that his home town of Brittany, France, had a similar phantom light, was not surprised by their wariness. He admitted that the people back home "said their prayers a little better" whenever their own light appeared.

An editorial in the December 3, 1938 edition of the *Regina Leader-Post* gave voice to those who were not quite so prepared to believe that the Tabor Light was of supernatural origin.

> One may suggest that in due course a natural
> and scientific explanation will be forthcoming
> concerning the now famed "Tabor light" in the
> neighbourhood of a cemetery in the general Esterhazy,
> Sask. district. We are living in an age in which
> there is a demand for scientific explanation for
> much. Some who hew to the argument that this is
> a universe moving and evolving without the direction
> of supernatural power insist that in due course
> there will be scientific explanation of even mysteries
> touching the traditionally unknown.

Indeed, much of the interest in Old Faithful was on behalf of those who adopted the challenge to disprove it as a phantom. Scientific theories abounded.

Several people loosely dismissed the light as a "will-o'-the-wisp" or flammable gases found above marshes or graveyards as a result of organic decomposition. A reporter at the *Regina Leader-Post* dealt briefly with this idea, in the December 1, 1938 edition:

> Theorists have laid the cause to rotted trees,
> phosphorus in the moonlight, or the presence of
> gas or oil throwing up a glare. Always, though,
> the theories are dashed when the impish glow appears
> from another spot.

The *Leader-Post's* December 3, 1938 edition quoted one variation on that theme, coming from a Chinese resident of Assiniboia who claimed to have experienced similar phenomenon in his homeland. He attributed the light to the decay of bodies and decomposition of their blood. Over time, he reasoned, this process would release a gas that was phosphorous in nature. "It would seem this gas finds its way to the surface and spontaneously bursts into a small light and gradually into a larger light and then disappears," he said, never explaining how these gases would have moved outside the periphery of the cemetery, where the light was always seen, or how they would move, sometimes with the speed of a vehicle, along the road.

Some people suggested that the light may be the land-faring equivalent of St. Elmo's Fire, a luminous form of corona discharge sometimes seen in the sails of early sailing vessels. What they couldn't address was how such a rare phenomenon which had only before been witnessed at sea could appear frequently, in the same spot, on dry prairie land.

One of the more popular scientific theories seemed as fantastic as the superstitions it was attempting to replace. The idea presented was that the light was nothing more than an owl with phosphorus wings. In the December 9, 1938 edition of the *Regina Leader-Post*, under the headline "LIGHT SCARES PEOPLE," one man ridiculed that notion:

> D.D. Selkirk of Spy Hill, Sask. is one of those
> who do not believe the ghostly light near Tabor
> is an owl with phosphorescent wings. He says no
> owl would fly around the same place for 30 years,
> that the bobbing ball of fire always sticks to the
> road, that an owl would not, and that it has come
> to within two or three feet of people before it
> would vanish. People at three feet would be able
> to distinguish an owl, even on the darkest night,
> especially if it was "lighted up" by phosphorus.

One brazen sceptic managed to grab a front-page headline for himself, when he announced that he had a plan to trap the Tabor Light in a specially designed mesh wire basket. He bragged that if he concealed himself, holding this "trap" on the end of a long stick, he could quickly catch the light within it. He was quite sure that what he would find in the basket was a swarm of small swamp flies or gnats, his "scientific explanation" of the light. No subsequent article in the newspaper suggested he was ever successful.

It may be reasonable to assume that he simply changed his mind, as there are several accounts of sceptics who did a dramatic about-face after witnessing the light themselves. In one case, a police officer from Esterhazy was travelling the cemetery road when he saw a light approaching. Thinking it was a motorist with a burned-out headlight, he leaned out the window of his vehicle, preparing to stop the approaching car. Much to his surprise, when the light came closer, he saw that there was no automobile supporting it. The officer stared at the apparition in shock, as it bounced right past him on the road and eventually disappeared.

Whether people believed the light to be of supernatural origin or a natural anomaly, the fascination grew. So did the crowds, and eventually the iron gates to the Tabor Cemetery were barred, to stop the desecration of graves. The nightly vigils continued, but were confined to the roadside.

Amid the commotion, there were suspicions raised about the people of the area in December of 1938, when officials and stenographers at the Prairie Farm Rehabilitation headquarters in Regina announced that letters coming from the Esterhazy district had been marked with a mysterious and fearsome crab-like emblem. There was brief speculation that residents of the region had cultishly adopted this insignia as their impression of the Tabor Light, but it faded when the sketch stopped appearing. More than likely, this was simply a joke, perpetrated by someone who had access to Esterhazy's mail.

At the height of its popularity, the Tabor Light inspired a fair bit of playfulness. James Brown, the proprietor of the hotel in Esterhazy, was confused one month when his power bill arrived. There was an additional charge levied for consumption of light made by the will-o'-the-wisp after midnight. Eventually, Mr. Brown decided that the folks at Canadian Utilities in Calgary were just having a little fun with him.

Unfortunately, what was fun for some was a source of real fear for others. Farmers in the district truly believed that the frequent appearances of the light meant that doom was at their doorsteps. It was taken as a warning that something sinister was fated to occur in the area. Aggressive types ignored the fact they knew not what they were dealing with, and organized armed patrols and volunteer watches by the cemetery at night. As worry spread, a local Catholic priest by the name of Father J. Pirot suggested a form of spiritual protection. He told people that if they saw the light, to simply pray for the souls of those buried in Tabor. It was the second time in thirty-three years that he had offered that advice.

Father Pirot had been the priest at the Kaposvar church just north of Esterhazy for thirty-five years. He had the perspective of someone who had lived in the area since the very first sighting of Old Faithful, and the perspective of a spiritual man. Perhaps that is why he was interviewed by the *Regina Leader-Post* on December 1, 1938.

In the course of the interview, Father Pirot hinted at a connection between the phantom light and the early, anti-religious sentiment of the cemetery's founders. But he claimed he could offer no further explanation. "The light is there," he added, "but what it is I do not know; it comes from the cemetery and that cemetery is certainly a great mystery."

On December 10th, just nine days after his comments appeared in the newspaper, Father Pirot changed his story in a startling confession to his congregation. On December 11th, in a letter addressed to His Grace Archbishop Monahan of Regina, he documented this confession. It was the revelation of a secret he had kept for thirty-three years; that he, Father J. Pirot, was responsible for the very existence of the Tabor Light.

Father Pirot had come to the small church at Kaposvar in 1903, just as the anti-religious fervor was hitting its highest pitch. He found many of the Bohemian families living east of Esterhazy divided; often the men had been reading atheistic literature and were turning their backs on their faith, while the women still struggled to take their children to church and instil religious values.

In one such family a little girl died. The father refused a Christian service for her, maintaining that she had no soul. Despite her grieving mother's pleas, the girl was buried unceremoniously in the Tabor Cemetery. It was 1905.

The mother despaired constantly over her dead child, and turned to Father Pirot for consolation. To ease her distress, he assured her that he would do what he could for the girl through prayer, and he kept his word. That very day, he made the eighteen-mile journey from Kaposvar to Tabor, and by the side of the road, he prayed.

According to Father Pirot's confession, he prayed not only for the soul of the girl, but for a sign from God that she indeed had a soul. He prayed for a sign for the people – not in the cemetery, where they would fear it to be a ghost – but on the road, for all to see. Within days came the first reports of the Tabor Light, and for the first time, Father Pirot encouraged people who saw it to pray for the souls of those buried in Tabor. Thirty-three years later, as fear spread and farmers talked of selling out to escape the scourge that would surely befall them, he felt it necessary to share the decades-old secret of his petition to God.

Was Father Pirot responsible for the Tabor Light? If so, why did he keep his involvement a secret for so long, particularly when the light, in his view, was being so clearly misinterpreted? Was the story an invention, perhaps to calm growing fears and keep people from pulling up stakes and starting over elsewhere? Only one thing is certain; Father Pirot told two very different versions of the story – one to his congregation and to His Grace Archbishop Monahan, and quite another in the interview he granted the *Regina Leader-Post*. Not particularly priestlike behavior, but perhaps he could be excused, given the highly unusual circumstances of his situation.

Today, the Tabor Light remains well-known to locals, if not as dramatically active as it was in the late years of the Depression. Perhaps in true celebrity-style, it will one day make a comeback.

We can hope.

There is no reason why Saskatchewan should not be full of ghost stories. Contrary to what some people think, ghosts do not need old cultures, old houses, or romantic old-world settings. Not only did immigrants bring their ghosts with them when they came to the New World, but ghosts readily sprout wherever people settle.

Michael Taft
Folklorist and Author
August 14, 1994

PASQUA LODGE; RUMOURED TO BE THE MOST HAUNTED BUILDING
AT THE ECHO VALLEY CONFERENCE CENTRE.

Spirits of the San

Four kilometres north of Fort Qu'Appelle, by the shores of Echo Lake, is one of Saskatchewan's most unique and historic sites. Today, this collection of buildings is known as "The Echo Valley Conference Centre"; a scenic, comfortable and affordable location for events ranging from weddings to corporate workshops. In years past, it was known for a very different purpose, and by a different name.

This is the story of Fort San.

Tuberculosis. They called it "the white plague," and "the Captain of all the men of death."

In this age of antibiotics and AIDS, it is difficult to imagine how a diagnosis of this bacterial infection used to terrify. Until the 1944 discovery of the drug streptomycin, however, thousands of tubercular Canadians every year suffered horrible deaths.

MANY OF THE ROOMS APPEAR AS THEY DID DECADES AGO.

Before drug therapy, the weapons medical science had to wield against the disease were few and unimpressive by today's standards. There was bed rest, wholesome food and plenty of fresh air, no matter how low the thermometer mercury dipped. There were a few crude surgical techniques. And there was isolation; not for the good of the patient, but to prevent spread of the disease. To meet all of these needs, sanatoriums, or "sans," as they were often called, sprang up around the country. In Saskatchewan, Fort San was the first.

Although plans for Fort San began in 1911, it wasn't until the end of the First World War that construction was completed. Many tubercular veterans came home in need of treatment, and this patriotic issue lent appeal to the funding drive. 1919 saw the facility finally open, with returning soldiers occupying over half the available beds.

But if World War I helped build Fort San, World War II helped render it obsolete. Out of that conflict came the advent of antibiotics, an effective treatment for tuberculosis. As the quality of the drugs improved, the need for sanatoriums diminished, and eventually, all treatment could be handled in hospitals.

In 1972, Fort San closed its doors, and the grounds were sold to the provincial government for the princely sum of one dollar. The joke – according to Gus Vandepolder, who now manages Echo Valley Conference Centre – is that the province got taken. Fort San, essentially an autonomous village of some fifty buildings, was expensive to maintain, and for years it was of little use.

In the eighties, the property began serving some purpose, as a summer school of the arts and the site of an occasional convention. It still operated at a huge deficit, however, and buildings began to fall into disrepair. Fort San was in danger of closing permanently when, in 1992, Saskatchewan Property Management Corporation began negotiating with the Department of National Defence. The latter agreed to move their Western Canadian Sea Cadet Training Program to Echo Valley, providing a much-needed major tenant and a new lease on life. Guaranteed income from the Cadets each summer finally prompted the government to refurbish the site.

Today, the place has the appearance of a well-tended time capsule. Stroll down the red and green checkered tile of the hallways, past old-fashioned windows and hospital-white walls, and it's easy to imagine the year is 1940. Take a moment in any of the Spartan rooms, and you'll find yourself believing that just that morning, patients on hospital beds were wheeled through the broad doorways leading to the sun balconies, where wide-flung windows brought them their fresh-air cure.

There is a sense of time being absorbed here, and according to

SOME HALLWAYS REMAIN SO HOSPITAL-LIKE, ITS NO WONDER THE
GHOST OF "NURSE JANE" IS CONTENT TO ROAM THEM.

some, more remains of the past than just old-fashioned fixtures and furniture.

Over the years, Fort San gained a reputation as a haunted place. There were rumours of entire floors appearing to be lit up and bustling with activity, when in fact, they were empty and deserted. People gossiped about patients and orderlies from a previous era roaming the halls, late at night. Isolated and antique, with a dramatic history, Fort San was Saskatchewan's version of a ghost-ridden castle.

One of the first stories I heard of Fort San came from a man who had attended a summer music camp there, in the late seventies or early eighties. On a particularly warm day, every band member had gathered on the lawn for practise. One young man realised that he had forgotten something in his room, and ran back to the deserted lodge to retrieve it. As he dug through his luggage, he was distracted by the sound of singing.

It was a woman's voice, high and clear; and confusing, since this was the lodge assigned to the men. The voice was accompanied by the sound of running water, likely coming from the bathroom across the hall. The young musician walked over to the doorway, where he could see clearly across to the line of porcelain sinks.

It was a woman, young and pretty, in a rather conservative dark dress that fell past her knees. The taps were running, and as she washed, the woman dreamily considered her reflection in the mirror. The young man called out to her politely.

"Excuse me, ma'am. I think you're in the wrong lodge. This is the men's."

She gave no indication of having heard him. Thinking that perhaps the running water had masked his voice, he spoke up.

"Excuse me? Lady?"

Instead of turning towards him, the woman backed away from the sink, and out of his range of vision. He decided to approach her, and walked the half-dozen steps across the hall to the bathroom.

In that time, she had vanished.

The young man was perplexed, but not frightened at first. He stood in the bathroom trying to reason how the woman could have left his sight so quickly, how she could possibly not be in the bathroom or the hallway. As he tried in vain to puzzle it out, what he noticed next *did* frighten him; every sink in the bathroom was completely dry.

Apparently, he rejoined his band-mates in a great hurry, and refused to go back to the lodge until later that evening, when it was comfortably filled with people.

I had also encountered rumours about a group of writers who had taken a Ouija board to their Fort San retreat. They were aware of the conference centre's supernatural reputation, and hoped to conjure some spiritual entertainment.

What actually happened that night is difficult to know; the participants are evidently, to this day, too upset to discuss the matter. I spoke to a man who had interviewed several of the people involved, and he would only say that the writers summoned much more activity than they bargained for, and had frightened themselves badly.

It seems they may have frightened others, as well. There was an alcoholics' rehabilitation group booked into Fort San on that same evening. The story has it that these poor people were terrified, sleeping two to a bed, completely unaware of what was causing the strange events around them, and probably suspecting hallucinations.

I relayed these stories to General Manager Gus Vandepolder, an affable man who made us instantly welcome. Gus found the tales interesting, but not surprising. He felt that the site's historical record made it irresistible fodder for superstitious types. And to add colour, of course, there are the grim statistics.

"On average, since 1919, forty people died here of tuberculosis, every year the place was open," Gus explained. "So that's a fair number of people to have expired on site. And then there are a variety of other stories people tell."

One person who tells those other stories well is Bernice Desjarlais. Gus introduced the trim, pretty woman, and let her perform the duty of tour guide. No one could have been a better choice.

Bernice has worked at Echo Valley Conference Centre for six years. Long before she joined the house-keeping staff, however, she was a tuberculosis patient who spent three of her precious childhood years confined to the "San."

"I was in here when I was six years old, for two years," she said matter-of-factly, adding later that her father had been a World War II serviceman who made it home before she did. "I came back in when I was twelve," she continued, "that time, for ten months."

Bernice went on to explain that a tubercular gland in her neck had burst during her first stay, very nearly killing her. A few years later, when her glands became swollen, she was rushed back to the sanatorium. After ten months of separation from her family and friends, they took the little girl's tonsils out, and sent her home. It had not been a recurrence, after all.

The result of those stays has been that Bernice knows every inch of every building on the site. She guided us up and down polished staircases, through passageways, and past every possible point of interest.

"This is where the babies were kept," she advised us at one point. In another area, she showed us where staff members went, when they were feeling ill. "I think there are even some pillows around here that are still stamped 'sick bay,'" she said.

At one point, she led us into a small green-tiled room. With the shy smile that often accompanied her nuggets of personal information, Bernice revealed that this had been an operating room. "This is where they took out my tonsils, in '49," she confided.

Bernice not only knew the landscape, she knew the legends. She informed us that Pasqua Lodge was the most haunted of all the buildings, explaining that when it was a sanatorium, "this lower floor is where all the very sick people lived."

"The treatment area was just down there," Gus offered by way of an explanation. Interestingly, while on the subject of convenience, so was the morgue.

Although she had been familiar with the facility since the 1940s, it wasn't until four years ago that Bernice became aware of the various ghosts.

"One day we were sitting having our coffee, after lunch," she said, "and a lady who was staying there [in Pasqua Lodge] came in and sat down with us. She asked us if we had ever seen anything. We said no, and she said, 'Well, I've just got one more night to sleep here, and I'll be happy to go home.' We asked her why, and she said that at three o'clock that morning, they were all awakened by this noise ... as though someone was dragging heavy chairs and slamming heavy doors and walking up and down the hallways. The upstairs people thought it was the ones downstairs, and vice versa. But nobody was doing anything. She said, every night, she would leave her door open just to watch. She was scared. She was waiting to go home," Bernice finished solemnly.

One commonly seen apparition at the Conference Centre is known as "Nurse Jane," or "Jane, the Folding Ghost"; the latter title inspired by the fact that she is frequently seen folding linens. On other occasions, she seems content to push a wheelchair around the premises. According to folklore, Jane was a distraught nurse who committed suicide while working at Fort San. Hopefully, she wasn't attempting to escape an unbearable job, for she now appears to have it for eternity.

When tuberculosis patients were moved from one location to another, wheelchairs were always used, so as not to interfere with the prescription of "rest." It's not surprising, then, that wheelchairs seem to be a common spectral theme.

Bernice pointed down a long hallway in Pasqua Lodge. "That doorway at the end," she waved her hand, "when the door was half shut, we used to see the shadow of a wheelchair on it." The ghostly shadow was apparently so distinct that it always drew someone down to investigate. By the time they'd reach the end of the hallway, however, the apparition would disappear.

Still on a medical theme, Bernice told us of another odd experience she had, decades after the buildings had been used as a treatment facility. "One morning I came to work and I found a nurse's cap on our desk in the laundry room," she said. After asking around to see if anyone wanted to claim the cap, she eventually took it home. "I thought 'well, souvenir!,'" she laughed. "Thought maybe I'd wear it for Hallowe'en." Instead, she felt strangely reluctant to keep the white cap, and took it back to work. "I put it in the kitchen," she said. "I don't know what became of it." Perhaps Nurse Jane reclaimed it.

Another eerie incident happened in what Bernice referred to as "one of the old buildings," one that has since been torn down. She had been making beds with some co-workers, and noticed on their way out of the building that a light had been left on at the end of the hallway. Bernice walked back and turned it off. "By that time, the girls were gone out the door," she explained. "I was coming back ... halfway down the hallway, and I heard 'click.' I looked back, and the light was on again. I didn't stay in there too long."

As interesting as the stories about the former sanatorium are people's reactions to them. Lending credibility to Bernice Desjarlais' testimony is the fact that she won't enter Pasqua Lodge alone, if at all possible. She is less hesitant if the place is littered with the comforting sight of people's belongings, but maintains that if working alone in Pasqua were her job, she would find another one.

A male employee who works nights at Echo Valley Conference Centre harbours even stronger feelings. According to Gus Vandepolder, this man is so completely unwilling to enter Pasqua alone after dark, he's even risked his job.

Gus assigned the man a small chore to take care of in Pasqua Lodge, one night, and noticed three days later that it hadn't been attended to. When Gus questioned the man, his explanation was that he hadn't been able to find a person available to accompany him.

"He'll give midnight tours to a group of people," Gus added, "but don't ask him to go in alone."

Gus Vandepolder's own feelings about the ghosts are interesting. He doesn't really think that anything spectral is roaming the halls. However, he's honest enough to admit that he occasionally gets "spooked."

"Doing my personal laundry here, a couple different nights, a door would suddenly close," he said. "I'd go investigate, and there'd be no one there. And there *should* be no one there, because the building's empty. Yet there's a slamming door ... I put it down to 'okay, there's a wind ...' I mean, I don't want to believe in ghosts. I have to work here."

Whether he believes in the phenomenon or not, Gus has a great appreciation for the entertainment value of the folklore, particularly the more colourful details.

"On your way up here, did you pass a sign that said 'Stiffville?'" he asked, with a smile. We nodded. "Mr. Stiff was the undertaker that used to attend to cases here," Gus explained. Mr. Stiff may have had an unfortunate combination of name and occupation, but it was interesting enough to earn him a place in *Ripley's Believe It or Not*, and respectable enough to name a nearby community.

Most of the folklore is much more morbid, though. I had heard stories of tunnels connecting the buildings, which were used to transport corpses in the dead of winter. Gus thought that was unlikely, explaining that they were actually service tunnels, used to maintain a network of utility pipes. Still, when I stared down one dimly lit passageway that emptied into the morgue, I felt a chill.

Another common bit of hearsay was expressed as a certainty by Bernice. As we were walking past some windows on the north side of Pasqua Lodge, she indicated the hills beyond. "Lots of times people died here, and they had no family," she said. "If nobody claimed the body, they'd get buried back there in the hills, with no marker."

Officially, there is no burial ground on site, yet this is one of the more persistent Fort San stories. Gus Vandepolder heard of one staff member finding a skull on the property, in 1992, and many people treat the unsubstantiated rumour as a simple matter of fact.

The idea is a central theme in Veronica Eddy Brock's novel, *The Valley of Flowers* (1987). While the book is a work of fiction, it is nonetheless rooted in truth, based on the author's own experience at Fort San. It is written several times in the novel that for every flower planted out by the gates, the heroine had heard that "a dead body was buried back in the hills." Although this has yet to be proven as anything more than a rumour, it is an impressively wide-spread and enduring one.

But it is little wonder that the dark stories persist. Fort San was a medical purgatory where hundreds died and thousands suffered. Isolation, loneliness and pain were a way of life for its citizens; some of whom lost years of their lives, if not life itself.

Today, the Echo Valley Conference Centre is a bustling, sunny,

118

accommodating alter-ego to the San. By all accounts, it is a pleasant and productive place to be. Why, then, the continued ghostly visitations?

They used to say it about tubercular spots on x-rays; these shadows take time to chase away.

AT THE REAR OF PASQUA LODGE IS THIS SMALL PORCH, REFERRED TO IN VERONICA EDDY BROCK'S 1987 NOVEL, *THE VALLEY OF FLOWERS*, AS "DEAD CENTRE." THE UNDERTAKER'S WAGON WOULD PULL UP TO THIS DOOR TO COLLECT BODIES FROM THE MORGUE, DIRECTLY BELOW.

The Yorkton Child

The city of Yorkton is celebrated as the home of North America's longest-running short film festival. Even before the festival's inception in 1950, however, it was locally known as the site of one of the province's better-known ghost stories.

She's just a little girl, four years old at the most, and people who see her for the first time are usually concerned that she's been left unattended. When they approach in order to question her, however, she disappears into thin air.

That is the child of the crossroads, a spirit that's haunted Yorkton for decades. This sporadic visitor never ages, and never does more than wander along the side of the road by herself.

The locals have no explanation for the little girl's appearance, but one woman I spoke to suggested that she may be a visitor from the city's nearby cemetery. Chances are, it will never be known why this child continues to materialize at the crossroads.

A Phantom at the Fort

THE OFFICER'S QUARTERS AT FORT BATTLEFORD. EARLY IN THE
CENTURY, A MAN ENDED HIS LIFE IN THIS BUILDING, PERHAPS ONLY
TO SPEND HIS AFTERLIFE TRAPPED THERE.

*The town of Battleford is nestled scenically between the North
Saskatchewan and Battleford rivers. It is a place steeped in history, having
been the original capital of the Northwest Territories and one of the major
theatres of conflict during the Riel Rebellion.*

*Interestingly, this ghost story is rooted in much calmer times. It was told
to me by a costumed guide at the impressive Fort Battleford.*

"As far as we know, George wasn't even here during the seige
in 1885," the woman explained. "He came out west a few
years later."

"George" was, according to our guide, a dental surgeon who had
been posted at the Fort in the late 1800s. Although he was fortunate
enough to have missed the violence of the Rebellion, the man must

have been tortured by terrible personal problems. Shortly after the turn of the century, George put a gun to his head and ended his life in an upstairs room of the Officers' Quarters.

If George was seeking escape from his dreary life at Fort Battleford, however, he may not have succeeded. There are several people who believe he is still there.

"It was very strange," the woman said. "There were always folks who would walk into the Officers' Quarters, then turn around and walk straight back out." It seems that some people became highly uncomfortable in the building; many would express having sensed the presence of another, when they were there alone.

Our guide admitted that despite many reports of the resident ghost, she devoted very little thought to George. Perhaps that explains why he singled her out for special attention.

"One morning I walked into the building to prepare for the day, and quite a bit of furniture had been overturned." The woman knew that no one had been in earlier than she, and that everything had been orderly when she locked up the night before. Being of a practical nature, she simply reorganized the room and set about her day's work.

On another occasion, the woman opened the Officers' Quarters in the morning to find playing cards arranged in bizarre patterns on the floor. The cards were a prop, set on a table to add some colour to the surroundings. George seemed to feel that they were more interesting when laid out on the creaky floor.

I asked our guide if all these events had invested her with a belief in the supernatural. She responded with a broad smile.

"Oh, I've *always* believed in ghosts," she said, and went on to explain that early each morning, she is wakened by the spirit of her dead grandmother; a woman who obviously disliked laziness.

"It's not at all frightening, but I can never sleep in," she laughingly complained.

She should count her blessings. Most people dealing with one ghost at work and another at home would have trouble getting any sleep at all.

A sign of changing times: Years ago, the staff at Fort Battleford who had had experiences with "George" were forbidden to tell visitors. Today, the rule has relaxed, and guides are allowed to add their own spooky stories to the historical ones they relay about the Fort.

The key word here is "belief." [Ghost stories] explore the boundaries of belief through the recounting of something which is not part of ordinary experience.

Michael Taft

Folklorist and Author

August 14, 1994

The Mysterious Mirror

The following four stories were researched and originally written by Dave Geary for the September-October 1994 issue of Broadway Magazine.

I have chosen to dramatize them for effect, and pseudonyms have been employed, but all facts regarding the supernatural phenomenon remain unchanged.

It was one of those cozy-looking family houses built on Taylor Street, in Saskatoon, back in the forties. It's war-time style qualified it as a "character home," and Janice Wynn was smitten enough to lay down a damage deposit.

"There's a beautiful archway, leading into the kitchen," Janice told her children, "and big windows to let in the sun." Best of all, in the small living room that was characteristic of homes of that era, there was a decorative mirrored wall. The reflection gave the illusion of openness, creating an inviting space that Janice was sure her family would enjoy.

Furniture was moved in and meticulously arranged. Pots and pans found new places in new cupboards, and clothing was hung in dark, empty closets. Within two hectic days, the Wynn family had settled in comfortably.

But the comfort was not to last.

In their old home, the living room had been the social centre for Janice and her children. It was where they watched television, worked on school assignments, read magazines or simply talked to one another. Now, although the family camaraderie seemed to be intact, no one stayed in the living room long enough to allow the whole group to gather.

Janice would walk into the room and sit down, and only moments later, someone would leave. Within a short time, Janice herself would feel restless and uncomfortably self-conscious, and would move to another room. This unusual rotation would continue for hours, with no one in the family really understanding why they felt so uneasy in the mirrored room.

One day, Janice's young daughter expressed what everyone had been feeling. The little girl had just barely settled down at the coffee table with her colouring books and crayons when she began gathering them up in frustration.

"I hate this place!" she cried, as she stomped off to the kitchen, "It always feels like when Holly's starin' at me!"

As a mother, Janice had stopped a hundred fights that began with the timeless phrase, "so-and-so is staring at me!" But on this occasion, the words hit home. That was the feeling; someone *was* staring at them when they sat in the living room. Nervously, slowly, Janice turned to the mirrored wall. She wasn't sure what she expected to see, but meeting nothing more than her own terrified gaze made her feel ridiculous.

"Oh, something in the mirror is watching us," she mocked herself, "How foolish!" Still, she could never shake the uncomfortable feeling that crept into her in that room.

Although they had now been there a few months, Janice stubbornly decided that the family was still adjusting to the move. After all, the baby, just eighteen months old, had been out-of-sorts for ages. Janice thought that moving his crib into her bedroom might soothe him, but the effect seemed to be the opposite. Day and night, if the child slept in that room, he woke up screaming or frantically babbling. When he slept in another room, the frightening behaviour stopped.

Eventually, Janice learned why.

As she was rolling over in bed, one night, Janice woke herself enough to sense that she was not alone in the bedroom. Thinking that one of her children had come looking for her, she fought back sleep and opened her eyes.

It was then she saw her; the vaporous white form of a woman moving towards the bed. Even more alarming, this apparition looked wildly angry, and in a malevolent gesture, stretched her hands out toward Janice's throat.

And then she was gone.

It rarely takes more than that to make someone feel unwelcome, and predictably, Janice began an immediate search for a new home.

Happily, she found one. Today the Wynn family is enjoying life in a cheerful house where nothing upsets the children, no fearsome spectres appear in the night, and a person can spend hours in the living room without sensing that someone, somewhere is watching.

It sounds infinitely more cozy than the strange house of mirrors on Taylor Street.

Two Families; One House

"Mom! Mom!"

Wanda Persky was standing at the kitchen sink when she heard the child cry out. It doesn't even startle me anymore, she thought, as she reached for a dish towel and turned around. Sure enough, through the open crack of a bedroom door, Wanda could see her playing.

She was a sweet little girl with her hair swept back in ribbons. The child crouched on the floor in her pretty pink dress, intent on some unseen toy or game.

"Mom! Mom!"

With a sigh, Wanda turned back to her dishes. It was unsettling, but there was nothing she could do. The child was not her daughter; she was not anyone's daughter in this lifetime. She was a ghost, and experience had taught Wanda that if she tried to approach her or answer her calls, the girl would simply disappear.

It had been years since the Persky family first moved into their Silverwood Heights home in Saskatoon, and years since they first met the spirits they were to share it with. The girl in the pink dress was a frequent visitor; so was a grown man with short hair and old-fashioned breeches. They were translucent figures, often appearing silhouetted in front of the windows. The girl could also be seen behind partially closed doors, and her appearances were frequently accompanied by the voice of a child calling its mother.

They were unusual tenants, these ghosts, but Wanda and her family had grown accustomed to their presence. For years, it was a harmonious cohabitation.

Unfortunately, it was not destined to remain as such.

The ghosts, who had established themselves as harmless apparitions, began to take on a physical quality. At first it was merely playful – the Persky children would feel someone tap them on the shoulder and turn to find no one there – but as time went on, the spectral "touches" became increasingly forceful and threatening. When Wanda's children began to be literally pushed around by the spirits, she felt it was time to do something. A Catholic priest was called, and persuaded to come by and bless each room of the house.

Since then, the supernatural activity has stopped. There have been no more shoves by invisible hands, no more children's voices calling for their mothers, and no more apparitions at the windows or anywhere else.

For the first time in nearly a decade, the Perskys have a home to themselves.

A Two-Storey Spook

There is a large house on Saskatoon's Lansdowne Avenue that was long ago divided into apartments, and in the early 1970s, Gary Stockwell lived in the one-bedroom unit, upstairs.

It was a nearly perfect place for him; spacious, inexpensive and comfortable. On the down-side, it wasn't particularly quiet.

On a regular basis, Gary was bothered by the heavy sounds of doors opening and slamming shut in the apartment below. It was a strange thing, since he knew that apartment was sitting vacant.

Even more confusing was the frequent stomping of boots coming up the stairs towards his door. When Gary would walk out to the staircase to see who was visiting him, the noise would stop immediately. No one was ever there, and it wasn't long before Gary came to accept that he was living in a haunted house.

It was a bit of a relief when a married couple moved into the noisy suite downstairs. Gary thought that listening to the natural sounds of his neighbours would be a comforting change, and hoped that the additional human tenants would help squelch whatever other presence occupied the house.

His hope was in vain.

If anything, the supernatural activity seemed to increase, and become more violent in nature. On one occasion, Gary was reading quietly in his bedroom, when three electrical wall outlets in the room shorted out and exploded simultaneously.

"That's just old wiring in an old house," a sceptical friend said later, when Gary spoke of the incident.

"Really?" mused Gary. "Even though there was nothing plugged in the sockets?"

Late one Sunday evening, Gary had just come through the main door of the house. Before he climbed the stairs to his apartment, he was stopped by the couple who lived directly below him. They were angry at his inconsideration, complaining about Gary banging loudly on their ceiling for the past two days.

"But it couldn't have been me," said Gary, holding up a small suitcase by way of an explanation. "I went to Regina for the week-end."

The husband and wife went pale at this; they'd apparently had other experiences which could not be rationally explained. Within two weeks, they had moved out.

Gary was hesitant to follow them; after all, this apartment suited his needs in so many ways. It was late one night, while in bed, that he made his final decision.

I'm definitely leaving, he thought. First thing in the morning, if not sooner. Even if I don't have a place to stay, I'm gone.

Of course, Gary may have been influenced by the events of the moment. He came to this firm decision when his bedroom door, suddenly and unexplainably, began opening and slamming shut.

Believing he'd rather not wait to see what was next on the haunting agenda, Gary Stockwell left the house on Lansdowne Avenue the very next day.

The Haunted Handprint

In 1974, the Olsen family moved an old house from Saskatoon to a piece of property they owned in the countryside.

They also moved a ghost.

When the Olsens purchased the home, they had no idea it was haunted. When they hauled it out of the city, not a single supernatural thing took place. But it wasn't long after they moved in that the senior occupant of the house made himself known.

Sandy Olsen was cooking dinner one day, while the rest of the family worked in the yard. A sudden, insistent tapping noise made her turn from the stove. Nothing seemed amiss in the kitchen, however, and since Sandy knew she was in the house alone, she assumed that she had simply heard the children playing along the outside wall. She turned back to her cooking.

Tap-tap-tap.

It was definitely an inside sound. That's just like someone was hitting the table with a ... Sandy's thought was arrested mid-sentence, as she turned to investigate. In fact, she forgot about the tapping altogether, when she saw a heavy china platter that had been sitting on a cabinet by the far wall come sailing across the room by itself. It crashed dramatically against the door frame, sending out a thousand hand-painted slivers.

That was the Olsens' introduction to the phantom they would eventually name "Eddie." And in all fairness, Eddie did not misrepresent himself in that initial meeting. He was, first and foremost, a noisy spectre.

Most of Eddie's appearances involved crashing, banging, or tapping sounds. One evening, the Olsens heard a thundering noise that they could only describe as a bowling ball, travelling across the roof of the outside verandah. On one of his quieter nights, Eddie simply materialized into a misty human shape, standing by the bathtub. And every visit, quiet or clamorous, was accompanied by what the Olsens politely referred to as "the indescribable odour."

Although all his appearances were memorable, in 1979, Eddie found a way to truly make his mark. Sandy Olsen went downstairs one morning to find a large wet handprint on the glass pane of a storm window. When she tried to wipe it off, the print remained.

Over fifteen years later, it still remains; a vivid sign that no matter who legally owns the house, Eddie possesses it.

(Regarding academia's reluctance to enter into more intensive research in the field of parapsychology.)

Remember, academics, and scientists in particular, have had a conditioning, a training that is very much against all this stuff. They haven't had courses in it, they don't know the data, they haven't read it, they haven't had access to it. It's harder for them to change their beliefs than it is for lots of other people.

Dr. Buddy Wynn, Parapsychologist
University of Regina
September 26, 1994

Foolish Fire

UNEXPLAINED LIGHTS ARE REPORTED TO HAVE BEEN SEEN IN A
NUMBER OF SASKATCHEWAN'S CEMETERIES.

They have been called Ghost Lights, Earth Lights, Ignis Fatuus and Will o' the Wisp. They have been seen over cemeteries, mountain ranges, railways, roads and lakes. Witnessed in thousands of locations, world-wide; they are unexplained, elusive, luminescent globes of spectral fire that have fascinated people for centuries.

The literal definition of the Latin term "Ignis Fatuus" is "foolish fire"; nevertheless, there are those who take this "foolishness" very seriously.

Late one night, a southern Saskatchewan farmer notices lights moving about in the neighbouring farm yard, which he knows to be deserted. He drives over to investigate, and is perplexed when he arrives to find no lights, no apparent source of light and, most strangely, no tracks in the freshly fallen snow.

Over a period of decades, several people in the Wapella district report a phantom lantern that follows them, late at night. There is no threat of a chase; instead, the light acts as an escort, keeping a comfortable distance away, and disappearing once the person is safe at home.

In the rural area outside of Yorkton, a group of men wait patiently at a crossroads for their friend, whose lantern they can see in the distance. The lantern light grows brighter as it approaches, and they urge the man to hurry, lest they be late reaching their destination. The bobbing light draws closer, and the men prepare to greet their friend. Instead, they freeze in shock as the lantern they have been watching passes between them and moves on. No one is carrying it.

These are a few examples of the many and varied experiences human beings have had with phantom lights.

Although they haven't been studied until recently, awareness of this mysterious phenomenon goes back centuries. Generally, early societies created explanations to fit their spiritual belief system; the Snohomish Indians described the lights as doors to other worlds, the Yakima thought they could divine the future, and Australian Aborigines, who called them *min-min-lights,* believed they were manifestations of dead or evil spirits.

Whatever they may be, over the years, Saskatchewanians have reported an alarming number of them.

At Woodlawn Cemetery in Saskatoon, on several consecutive mornings in the late 1960s, murky orange lights were witnessed floating above ground, and darting in and out of the trees. There appeared to be no logical explanation.

Much further north is Candle Lake, named by the Cree Indians, who frequently witnessed an inexplicable light dancing above the water's surface. The glow is always seen in the direction of the north shore, which is the site of a Native burial ground. The Cree believed the area to be haunted, and never settled there.

Several phantom lights – including the ones at Woodlawn Cemetery, Candle Lake and the famous Tabor Light (see page 100) – seem connected to graveyards or burial grounds. Others eschew traditional cemeteries, but still act as luminescent markers at scenes of foul play or accident.

In a story reminiscent of the St. Louis Ghost Train (see page 81), some residents of Saskatoon claim to have seen a phantom locomotive light along the Grand Trunk Line south of Diefenbaker Park. Also mimicking the St. Louis legend is the suspected cause: an engineer who was killed decades ago in a derailment.

In the small community of Watson, they tell a story of a light that appears over a murdered man's grave, signalling that he is not at rest, and in Dryboro Lake, a ghost light haunts the area where a lone rancher disappeared before the turn of the century.

Folklore has it that the man had gone into Assiniboia that day, and sold all his stock. He apparently returned to his ranch, but was never seen or heard of again. That night, his shack burned to the ground, but no trace of the rancher's body was discovered in the smoldering ruins. For decades afterwards, Dryboro Lake was home to a dancing phantom light, which always appeared within a one-mile radius of the rancher's home.

Much rarer is the phenomenon of lights that seem to serve some premonitory purpose.

In September of 1938, Trans Canada Airlines pilot Captain David Imrie made a strange sighting as he flew the night mail between Regina and Moose Jaw. What he saw appeared to be the navigation lights of an aircraft, but no such craft was flying that route on that night. Sadly, only a few weeks after seeing the "ghost plane," Captain Imrie himself died in a plane crash.

Forty-six years earlier, Dan McKenzie witnessed a similarly foretold tragedy take place nine miles south of Whitewood. It was a dark night, and Dan and his friend Bob McCaw were lying on the grass in Dan's front yard. They noticed a bright light travelling towards them from the east. Initially thinking it was a friend, they got up and walked towards what they thought was his lantern. At that point, the light travelled back the way it came.

The light zigged and zagged a bit, always staying about 100 yards in front of the two men. Eventually, it led them to Bob's father's house. There, it perched on the log stable while Bob and Dan went inside, somewhat unsettled and glad to be rid of their strange chaperone.

Moments after the men arrived, Bob's sister Lizzie asked him to go to Whitewood and fetch the doctor. It seemed that ten-year-old Sarah, the youngest McCaw sibling, was very ill.

Bob hitched a horse to his father's buckboard and went for help. When he returned from his eighteen-mile round trip with the doctor, he noticed that the light was still atop the log stable.

There it remained, until later that night, when little Sarah died.

It is interesting to note that although phantom lights appear at a variety of locations, and seemingly for a variety of reasons, there are certain common characteristics. Generally speaking, they are found only in remote areas. With rare exceptions, they remain at a distance from the viewer, and will often react to noises or other sources of light by drawing further away or disappearing altogether.

Likely the most fascinating common quality of these lights is that they appear to have some form of consciousness, or intelligence. They react to the movements of those who watch them, sometimes seeming to play games.

There are naturally a number of scientific theories that attempt to explain phantom lights. In many cases, there might be a source of light that can't be seen from the vantage point of the viewer; perhaps a train or automobile. The light might be reflected from a distance. Another possible cause is marsh gas, which is created by decaying organic matter and is combustible. In some parts of the world, researchers are even investigating seismic stresses beneath the earth as a cause, theorizing that they release small masses of ionized gas into the atmosphere near fault lines.

There are no logical explanations, however, for the reactive behaviour of so many of the lights. While it seems reasonable to accept that decaying organic matter in a cemetery may create a phosphorescent reaction, it is difficult to say how that seemingly "natural" globe of light can engage in a lively game of hide-and-seek among the trees.

The one certainty is this: Saskatchewan is full of these glowing mysteries. Whether they are of natural or supernatural origin remains to be proven, but hundreds of witnesses make it difficult to deny that they truly do exist.

With that in mind, it may be time to pay attention to the brave types who say there's no need to fear the dark. As a cautious alternative, however – let's keep a close eye on "the light."

The Legend of Old Wives Lake

OLD WIVES LAKE – ITS WATERS EVAPORATED, LEAVING ONLY A
SALT-ENCRUSTED DEPRESSION AND THE INTRIGUING LEGEND TO
WHICH IT OWES ITS NAME.

*According to its tourism department, the province of Saskatchewan
boasts 100,000 lakes. Odds are that at least one of them would be haunted,
and according to Native folklore, one is.*

It is the legend of Old Wives Lake; part of the oral history of the
Plains Indians. The story is that three elderly Assiniboine women
were trying to escape from a raiding party of Blackfoot. They ran
until they came to the edge of the lake, then tried in vain to swim to its
far shore. Tragically, they were drowned. From that point forward,
according to legend, their wails of torment were heard across the waters
at night.

Because of this sad story, "Old Wives Lake" was what this water had always been called. At some point, for reasons unknown, the name was officially changed to Lake Johnstone. In 1963 the original title, in keeping with the legend, was restored. Some twenty years later, however, the shallow body of alkalic water fell victim to some of the prairie's driest years. The lake began to evaporate, leaving wide expanses of salt flats behind.

Today, the bleached and barren lake bed has a grim post-apocolyptic appearance. Each puff of air is white with salt, and nothing grows on the shores but scrubby brown thistle. It's a lifeless sight, but when the wind blows, one has to listen. There is something mournful in the sound; something vaguely haunting.

Old Wives Lake may be a mere ghost of its former self, but the legend lives on.

The Mysterious Man in Black

Ghosts are, by definition, unexplainable. In Kindersley, Saskatchewan, however, resides one spectral fellow who seems to defy even the commonly accepted theories regarding hauntings.

The house was built in the early sixties, on a site where no dwelling had ever existed. Yet, by 1968, one of the bedrooms had become home to a ghost. It was mysterious even by supernatural standards; the appearance of this man in black.

The first to see the apparition was one of the daughters of the family that lived in the home. The girl awakened in the middle of the night when the pet cat she had been sleeping with suddenly bolted out of the room. As she opened her eyes, the cat was soon forgotten; for a complete stranger was poised on the foot of her bed. He was a man dressed all in black, from the tips of his shoes to the brimmed hat that perched on his head. He was staring at her with fixation, but eventually disappeared without a single word or action. The daughter managed to finally get back to sleep. The cat, perhaps showing more sense, never returned.

Some months later, the family had a male guest stay overnight in that same bedroom. Early the next morning, one of the sons went to wake the man and advise him that breakfast would soon be ready. The guest paused for a moment before acknowledging the invitation.

At the breakfast table, the man asked the boy about the stranger in the doorway. His question was reflected with a blank stare.

"The tall man, the fellow who was standing beside you when you came to wake me," he added, only to be met with total, confused silence from his hosts. He described the stranger as being dressed entirely in black, including a black hat, and he said that the man appeared to have abnormally long arms. The family assured their guest that no one fitting his description was in the house, and the boy remained quite certain that he had been standing in the bedroom doorway alone.

Within a year, there was another sighting of the black-clad man in that bedroom. A woman who was visiting woke one night to see the stranger walking along the side of her bed, towards the foot. He paused there a moment, reached out to briefly touch her, then disappeared. The woman left with equal haste and found another place to sleep for the remainder of the night. Later, she described the man as others had, with one exception: he appeared to her without a hat, sporting instead a rather long, grey brush cut.

Even in the unpredictable world of ghosts, this apparition is a curiosity. There are records of hauntings in relatively new buildings, but usually the spirit can be connected to a previous structure, on the same site. In *Some Canadian Ghosts* (1973), Sheila Hervey suggests that the man may have once lived in the room, and must be a "relatively recent entry into the world of ghosts." Her explanation continues that "If he were from another period in history, his interest would not likely be confined to that one specific room in the house."

Maybe. But then again, maybe not.

Could it be that the man in black is not attached to the room, but to something within in? There have been various accounts of objects being haunted, particularly antique pieces of furniture. For all we know, the gentleman could have been visiting his former bed frame, or a bookcase that once stood in his own hall.

Another possibility is the property itself. A pioneer who had owned and loved the land might be expected to roam around more freely, but what about a fellow who had, according to the necessities of early rural life, been buried there? It's not inconceivable that an unmarked grave may have occupied the space deep beneath that bedroom. The man's sombre clothing certainly would suggest burial dress.

Whatever his reason for existing, the spirit never caused the family any real trouble. They came to accept him as simply an unusual feature in their home; a mystery that to this day, remains unsolved.

Wanted: One Resident Ghost

In the course of researching this book, I requested a bit of information from the Prince Albert Historical Museum. The museum's manager, Ron Smith, came to my assistance by mailing out the required documents.

Enclosed with the papers was Ron's entertaining cover letter, humorously despairing the fact that while he would have loved to contribute a story of his own, he was having difficulty realizing his dream of "a resident ghost."

"I am ashamed to say that a city the size of Prince Albert is surprisingly void of ghosts," Ron Smith wrote, in September of 1994. "If for no other reason than it used to be a provincial hanging centre, it should be entitled to its fair share of haunts."

Determined to have that to which he feels entitled, Smith does his best to ignite spooky rumours about the museum. He speaks of phantom howling sounds in the towers, when the temperature dips particularly low, and of mysteriously rattling dishes and singing in the pipes. He'll soberly tell anyone that he gets chills when the museum closes for the season, and empties itself of comforting human company. He even goes so far as to conjecture that his supposed spirits are "friendly ghosts" who seem to "get excited, when we talk." But it's all for nought.

According to Smith, all his wishful thinking and conjuring is regularly deflated by co-workers he refers to as "the zealous ghost busters."

"As fast as I try to activate them, my 'buddies' do them in," he laments, citing one particular instance when Smith was able to convince a newspaper reporter to do a story on the museum's spirits, only to have one of the ghost busters capture half of the article for himself and his maddeningly logical explanations.

Not one to give up, Ron Smith promises that the Prince Albert Historical Museum would be "a haven for ghosts," should one choose to haunt it. There are numerous relics and artifacts to cling to, and plenty of interesting history to enact in this former fire hall.

Smith longs to have something lurking in his museum's tower. Surely, there's a ghost out there who longs for a home.

Put them together, and it would be a match made in heaven – or some other blissful, nearby dimension.

BIBLIOGRAPHY

Books

Anderson, Frank W. 1989. *81 Interesting Places in Saskatchewan.* Saskatoon: Gopher Books.

Brock, Veronica Eddy. 1987. *The Valley of Flowers.* Regina: Coteau Books.

Broughton, Richard S. 1991. *Parapsychology; The Controversial Science.* New York: Ballantine Books.

Clery, Val. 1985. *Ghost Stories of Canada.* Willowdale, Ontario: Hounslow Press.

Colombo, John Robert. 1988. *Mysterious Canada.* Toronto: Doubleday Canada Limited.

Crickett, Hazel. 1991. *Our Heritage History: Acadia, Bickleigh, Kildare.* Snipe Lake, Saskatchewan: Our Heritage History Book Committe.

Guiley, Rosemary Ellen. 1991. *Harper's Encyclopedia of Mystical and Paranormal Experience.* New York: HarperCollins Publishers.

Hervey, Sheila. 1973. *Some Canadian Ghosts.* Richmond Hill, Ontario: Simon and Schuster of Canada, Ltd.

King, Andrew. 1967. *Estevan; The Power Centre.* Saskatoon: Modern Press.

Skelton, Robin and Jean Kozacari. 1989. *A Gathering of Ghosts.* Saskatoon: Western Producer Prairie Books.

Tadman, Peter. 1992. *Shell Lake Massacre.* Hanna, Alberta: Gorman and Gorman Ltd.

PERIODICALS

Broadway Magazine: "Saskatoon: Mystery City," by Dave Geary. September-October 1994.

The Edmonton Journal: November 22, 1993.

The Estevan Mercury: July 1994.

The Prince Albert Daily Herald: June 1990; February 29, 1992; October 1992.

The Regina Leader-Post: September 28, 29 and 30, 1931; November 30 and December 1, 2, 3, 5, 6, 9 and 14, 1938; January 23 and 24, 1975; August 25, 1979; and October 27, 1990.

The Saskatchewan Herald: April 23, March 20 and March 27, 1885.

The Saskatoon Star-Phoenix: March 19 and 21, 1921; August 16, 17, 18, 19 and 21, 1967; October 31, 1990; November 1, 1991; and July 30, 1992.

The Western Producer: "The Ghost at Belle Plaine" by John E. Grosskurth, April 12, 1973; and "Mission Lake Ghost" by Hazel Jardine, October 1993.

ARCHIVAL SOURCES

Saskatchewan Archives Board
"The Tabor Light"; Taft Folklore Collection
File 82-36
Janet Scholz

Saskatchewan Archives Board
"The Tabor Light"; Taft Folklore Collection
File 80-29
Shelly Theaker

Saskatchewan Archives Board
"Supernatural Legends About the Sinnet Road"; Taft Folklore Collection
File 83-19
Susan Elliot